Uniforms & Equipment of the Czarist Russian Armed Forces in World War I

Uniforms & Equipment of the Czarist Russian Armed Forces in World War I

- INFANTRY
- ARTILLERY
- GUARDS
- COSSACKS
- CAVALRY
- AIR SERVICE
- CZAR NICHOLAS II

Spencer Anthony Coil

Schiffer Military History
Atglen, PA

ACKNOWLEDGMENTS

First, and foremost, I would like to acknowledge and dedicate this work to all those who served in the Great War, especially those who appear in these photographs, and above all to my family, who supported and stood by me every step of the way, especially my ***Mother***, ***Aunt Frankie***, and ***Grandmother***!

I would like to thank the following individuals who directly or indirectly assisted in the creation of this work:

Steve Smith Studios (professional photographers)
The Agapova Family (historians, enthusiasts and linguists)
The Ezzo Family, especially Dipl. Ing. Blahad Ezzo (experts and enthusiasts)
The Gelfand Family (enthusiasts and linguists)
The Pomeranzeva-Halikin Family (historians, experts, enthusiasts and linguists)
The Hornkohl Family (enthusiasts)
The Otte Family (enthusiasts)
Alexei Grichine (expert, specialist and enthusiast)
Frau Dr. Grafin Irene Montjoye and her son Herr Mag. Graf Douglas Montjoye
(authors, journalists, enthusiasts, historians)
Dan Eibeck (historian, expert, specialist, enthusiast, archaeologist)
Mag. Clemens Ellmauthaler (historian, expert, specialist, enthusiast)
Fulvio Rizzo (historian, expert, specialist, enthusiast)
Professor Del Schwinke
President Dr. David Harpool
President Dr. Wil Goodheer
Vice President Dr. L. Boyer
All my friends in Estonia and the Russian Federation especially, Juri and Sergei!
(experts, specialists, enthusiasts)
Salvatore Vasta, uniform specialist, founder and curator of the Italian Front Group.
(www.italianfront.com)
Frédéric Gouraud (expert, specialist, enthusiast)
Mikhail Bereslavski (expert, specialist, enthusiast)
My Students

A special thanks to internationally acclaimed and recognized military medals and decorations experts, specialists, and enthusiasts, Herr und Frau Mag. Hartmut und Christine Rochowanski, who have maintained an impeccable reputation for over thirty years, and Franz Zabernig and family.

Book design by Ian Robertson.

Library of Congress Control Number: 2004112379

Printed in China.
ISBN: 0-7643-2157-9

We are interested in hearing from authors with book ideas on related topics.

Published by Schiffer Publishing Ltd.
4880 Lower Valley Road
Atglen, PA 19310
Phone: (610) 593-1777
FAX: (610) 593-2002
E-mail: Info@schifferbooks.com.
Visit our web site at: www.schifferbooks.com
Please write for a free catalog.
This book may be purchased from the publisher.
Please include $3.95 postage.
Try your bookstore first.

In Europe, Schiffer books are distributed by:
Bushwood Books
6 Marksbury Avenue
Kew Gardens
Surrey TW9 4JF
England
Phone: 44 (0) 20 8392-8585
FAX: 44 (0) 20 8392-9876
E-mail: Info@bushwoodbooks.co.uk.
Free postage in the UK. Europe: air mail at cost.
Try your bookstore first.

Contents

Introduction

The uniforms and equipment of the Czarist Russia Forces were as diverse as the nationalities of the soldiers serving in them. Although diverse, certain items were common or found essential by all soldiers serving in the armed forces.

Most soldiers wore some style of *gymnastiorka* (field blouse). The cut and style was simple, resembling the garb worn by Russian country folk throughout the empire. In photos of enlisted rank soldiers they appear to have been recruited directly from some small village in the countryside, the only military aspect of their appearance being shoulder boards on their upper body garments, which may or may not bear regimental numbers or unit distinctions.

A *gymnastiorka* (singular) was a high or low-collared field blouse that buttoned halfway down and pulled over a soldier's head. *Gymnastiorki* (plural) could be found with or without breast pockets, and were tailored from various materials, such as cotton, linen, leather, oilcloth, or wool. Most *gymnastiorki* were greenish brown or white in color. However, due to the various dyes used, colors of *gymnastiorki* varied. If a soldier wore his *gymnastiorka* in the field for an extended period, the elements as well as numerous launderings would alter the color. *Gymnastiorki* were either depot issued or privately made or purchased. Industry during this period in Russia was poorly organized and inadequate; therefore, many soldiers made their own *gymnastiorka* in addition to other uniform items, such as *sapogi* (boots), belts, trousers, and caps. Homemade items adhered loosely to regulations and varied in materials and colors. There were many interpretations as to how a *gymnastiorka* should fit on a soldier. Some soldiers wore the *gymnastiorka* very snug fitting, while others—particularly enlisted rank soldiers—preferred it belted and loose fitting. Officers, NCOs, and soldiers serving in guard units often detailed the cuffs and button flaps of their *gymnastiorki* with cloth piping of some sort. Other details that could be added to a *gymnastiorka* included various makes and manufactures of buttons, such as those bearing a Romanov double-headed eagle motif or a unit marking.

Just as *gymnastiorka* resembled the national garb of the Russian country folk, so did the headdress, such as the *furashka* (singular), or visor cap, and *papaha*, or fleece/fur winter cap, also referred to as astrakhan. *Furashki* (plural) were made of various materials, such as wool, linen, or cotton, and varied in size and shape. A popular style, particularly with officers and NCOs, was to stiffen the *furashka* with either starch, cardboard, or wire. Photos of soldiers taken later in the war show more soldiers preferred the *furashka* to have a crushed or collapsed appearance. *Furashki*, particularly those of enlisted rank soldiers, were lined with burlap, linen, or cotton, and were usually stamped with a date or manufacturer. The *furashki* worn by Officers and NCOs were usually lined with leather or silk. It was not uncommon for a *furashka* to have no lining at all, or even to have been homemade. The visor of a *furashka* was made of either leather or pressed cardboard-like material. Leather visors were normally left in their natural color. Those visors made from the pressed cardboard-like material were usually painted black. Many soldiers painted their visors a greenish brown, or a color that better matched the material of the *furashka*. Many, but not all, *furashki* had leather chins straps, which were often painted as well.

The *papaha* (singular) came in many different cylindrical shapes and was mainly worn in cold weather. Depot-issued *papahi* (plural) were made of cloth covered with curling ringlets of wool, and usually had quilted linings with issue stamps. The cloth of the *papahi* varied in color, while the curling ringlets of wool covering it were either black, white, gray, or a mixture of all three colors. The sides of the *papaha* could be unhooked and rolled down over a soldier's ears and neck to offer added protection in harsh weather. Like the *furashki*, *papahi* could be stiffened with either starch, cardboard, or wire, or left crushable and foldable. Cossacks and soldiers serving in Siberian regiments preferred black oversized, extra wooly *papahi*, which were usually homemade and often did not have the sides that unhooked.

The *papaha* and the *furashka* could easily be transformed from civilian to military headdress by fastening on a cockade or badge. Cockades were usually oval shaped or circular with black and orange roundels, and made of metal or porcelain. Officers and NCOs preferred metal or porcelain rosette cockades, while enlisted rank soldiers preferred the flatter die stamped metal ones. A cockade was either stitched or fastened on like a brad. It was common practice amongst soldiers to camouflage their cockades by stitching a piece of cloth over them. Badges, such as a Militia Cross or a Romanov double-headed eagle, were more difficult to camouflage, but were not worn on the front as often as the cockade. The Militia Cross was worn by volunteers, reservists, and national guardsmen, or by those who had served in these branches prior to active service. Militia crosses varied in shape, size, and manufacture, and had numerous styles of fasteners. Militia Crosses were normally die stamped metal, however, other materials were also used. Romanov double-headed badges were usually gilded and varied in shape, size, and manufacture. Most were maker marked and had a screw back or brad fastener.

In addition to the *papaha* and the *furashka*, other headdress, such as the *ushanka* and the *pilotka*, were worn. Like the *papaha*, the *ushanka* was a fleece or fur cap that was worn in cold weather. However, the *ushanka* differed in construction, in that the side flaps tied or buttoned together on top of the cap instead of unhooking from the front flap of the cap. The *pilotka* were either pillbox or tent-shaped forage caps. *Pilotka* were either greenish-brown, dark green, or the color of a particular regiment, and were made from various materials, such as wool, cotton, or linen.

Another item common to soldiers serving in the Czarist Russia armed forces was the wool overcoat, or *shinel* (singular). Cuts and styles of *shineli* (plural) varied, however, most photos from the period show soldiers wearing a double-breasted *shinel*. Officers, NCOs, and soldiers serving in Guard units often detailed the cuffs and button flaps of their *shineli* with various cloth piping. Other details that could be added to a soldier's *shinel* included various makes and manufactures of buttons, such as those bearing a Romanov double-headed eagle motif or a unit marking.

Shineli were depot-issued, or privately tailored or purchased by all ranks. Most depot issued *shineli* were made of a heavy grade of coarse greenish brown wool and had very rough-cut edges. Normally, rectangular wool collar patches bearing a regimental color were stitched to the collar of a soldier's *shinel*.

In addition to the *shinel* there was the *polushubok*, a long overcoat with a large chest pocket that buttoned shut. A *polushubok* was made from a heavy cotton or wool, and was usually lined with wool fleece or fur. This type of overcoat was preferred by officers and NCOs.

Often a soldier would fasten on shoulder boards, or *pogoni* (plural), to his *shinel* or *polushubok*, in addition to having a pair fastened on his *gymnastiorka*. *Pogoni* were made of wool and came in various shapes, lengths, and styles. Officers and NCOs generally preferred to wear stiff wool *pogoni* with ornate gold stitching displaying their regiment, rank, and unit distinctions. However, the most common style of *pogoni* were reversible, which were made of two pieces of rectangular-shaped wool stitched together, with one end that stitched to the edge of a soldier's shoulder, while the other end buttoned on. One side of the *pogoni* was in a regiment color—such as blue or red—while the other side was a greenish-brown. Regiment numbers, rank, and unit distinctions were usually stitched or stenciled on; however, a soldier could also obtain metal numbers and unit insignia that could be stitched or pinned to either side of their *pogoni*. Many photographs exhibit soldiers using a combination of all the aforementioned means of decorating their *pogoni*.

Unit insignia motifs differed depending upon the branch of service. For example, soldiers in the air service wore winged propellers on their *pogoni*; pioneers, a crossed shovel and axe; railroad troops, a crossed axe and anchor; balloonists, a winged anchor; artillerists, crossed cannons; grenadiers, a flaming ball; motorized troops, a winged wheel; machine gun troops, a machine gun; communication troops, two interlocking lightning bolts; naval troops, an anchor; and various other motifs, depending upon when and how the unit was formed.

In addition to displaying a soldier's regiment, rank, and unit, *pogoni* also served other functions, particularly when stitched on a *shinel*. *Pogoni* on a *shinel* helped hold a soldier's wool hood or cowl in place. A soldier's hood or cowl was referred to as a *bashlik*, and was typically tucked under a soldier's *pogoni* and belt, which held it in place while on a march.

The empire was composed of many different ethnic groups and nationalities. The armed forces depended upon these groups to help fill the ranks, either in the reserves or the frontline. Therefore, much latitude was granted, and various interpretations were permitted for Cossacks, Caucasians, and other irregulars who wore their traditional garb and furnished much of their own equipment. For example, Cossacks—amongst the finest cavalry in the empire—were apportioned vast areas of the best lands by the Czar in return for 20 years of military service. Among the traditional garments of a Cossack was a *tcherkessa*, which was a long coat or tunic usually made of wool. Across the chest of the *tcherkessa* were cylindrical cartridge pouches known as *gaziri*. *Gaziri* were either very plain or intricately crafted from brass or silver. Various styles and cuts of *tcherkessi* and *gaziri* were also worn by Caucasian and other irregulars.

Some of the traditional edged weaponry of these groups were the *kinjal* and the *shaska*, and were often carried by other soldiers, as well. A *kinjal* was a long knife with a double-edged blade, and a *shaska* was a curved saber. Both of these edged weapons had very distinctive grips that were often finely detailed.

Production of uniforms and equipment was adversely impacted by economic and political factors during the reign of the Czar. An example of a political factor can be seen in the self serving interests of most heads of state, such as overspending on personal needs rather than allocating state funds to industries critical to national defense. An example of an economic factor is seen in the inadequate production and distribution of not only uniforms and equipment, but also munitions. This led to the armed forces' dependence on imports from other countries to assist in equipping, as well as many troops being responsible for outfitting and equipping themselves.

Chapter One

Machineguns

A pre- to early-war Machinegun Company (pulemjótnaja róta) on maneuvers in southern Russia. The heavy iron-plated carriage provided protection, however, it proved to be too cumbersome to maneuver.

Two Maxim M1905 7.62mm machineguns captured by the k.u.k (imperial and royal) Austro-Hungarian army on the southwest front. This photo displays two of the various ways the M1905 could be mounted. In this particular photo one is mounted on a block of wood; the other is mounted on a two-wheel iron Sokolov carriage. 1916.

A group of frontoviki (frontline troops) manning two Maxim M1905 7.62mm machineguns mounted on a two-wheeled iron Sokolov carriage with armored shields. The frontoviki seen here wear wool overcoats (shineli) and French Adrian-style steel helmets with Romanov double-headed eagle badges. Riga, Latvia (Baltic State/Country), 1917.

Above: These soldiers are preparing to fire their Maxim M1905 7.62mm machinegun. Riga, Latvia (Baltic State/ Country), 1915.

Left: A Maxim M1910 7.62mm machinegun mounted on a Sokolov carriage with an armored shield. Moscow, 1917.

A group of machinegunners loading their Maxim machinegun on the southwest front in 1916.

A machinegun company (pulemjótnaja róta) poses with their Maxim M1905 7.62mm machineguns in a forest near the Masurian Lakes, 1914.

A studio photo of a Latvian machinegunner. The machinegunner insignias on his shoulder boards (pogoni) are die-stamped metal (machinegun motifs). Cloth insignias were also used, or machinegun motifs were painted on the shoulder boards. The machinegunner wears a sherst (wool) gymnastiorka (field blouse). The vertical cloth stripe running down the length of his button flap was characteristic for soldiers in the Guard units. Above the lower button on his gymnastiorka on the right is an orange and black ribbon, indicating he has been awarded the St. George Cross for valor. Pinned on his gymnastiorka is also a Latvian rifleman badge. Riga, Latvia (Baltic State/Country), 1915.

German soldiers watch as their Russian Kriegsgefanger (prisoner of war) carries his Maxim M1905. This photo is dated 1916.

Russian Kriegsgefangener (prisoners of war) in rough-cut overcoats pose around their Maxim M1905 machineguns.

A soldier of the k.u.k. (imperial and royal) Austro-Hungarian army leading a group of Russian Kriegsgefangener (Prisoners of War), 1916.

German soldiers wearing their pickelhaube (spiked helmets) escort Russian Kriegsgefangener (prisoners of war), 1914.

This is an official photo taken from a series produced in 1914 to fund the War. The Cyrillic inscription reads "No. 17 A machinegun pack-mounted."

This is an official photo taken from a series produced in 1914 to fund the War. The Cyrillic inscription reads, "No. 50 Machinegun platoon on the move."

This is an official photo taken from a series produced in 1914 to fund the War. The Cyrillic inscription reads, "No. 20 Loading rounds into a machinegun belt or belt feeding."

Chapter Two

Medical

A studio photo taken in Moscow in 1915. The medic enjoying his cigar wears a papaha (astrakhan or fleece/fur winter cap) made of a heavier wool than the ones issued. Soldiers in Siberian Regiments or Cossacks normally wore this style of papaha. The medals he wears on his heavy brownish gray wool overcoat (shinel) are a 1904 Russo-Japanese War period medal with the Cyrillic inscription that translates "God will take you when your time has come," (left), and a Czar Nicholas II Romanov commemorative medal (right). Both of these medals were awarded often and were very popular to wear.

A photo taken in 1916 at a studio in Nizhni-Novogorod. The medical NCO on the left wears a privately purchased khaki green wool tunic. He is easily identified as a medic because of the red crosses on his shoulder boards, cockade, and armband. The soldier on the right wears a thick cotton gymnastiorka, or field blouse. This gymnastiorka has an unusual cut, in that it buttons straight up with hidden buttons, instead of off to one side with exposed buttons. His cockade has been subdued or camouflaged, which was normally done with either paint or cloth. His shoulder boards (pogoni) indicate he is in Siberian Rifle Regiment No. 54.

Above: Nurses and surgeons from the Imperial Russian Red Cross, 1916.
Above left: The medical officer in this studio photo wears a papaha (astrakhan or fleece/fur winter cap) and a leather jacket with wool pogoni (shoulder boards) bearing medical insignia.
Below left: The medic in this studio photo is ready for the frontlines! He wears a double breast-pocketed privately tailored gymnastiorka (field blouse) and a camouflaged Red Cross armband made of wool.

This photo was taken in a studio in Moscow in 1914. All three soldiers seen here wear issue furashki (field caps) and gymnastiorki (field blouses). The soldier seated on the right wearing the medic armband wears a 1904-1905 Russo-Japanese War period medal with the Cyrillic inscription that translates, "God will take you when your time has come."

This group of soldiers wears the pre- to early-war dark green wool tunic. This group also displays a wide variety of ranks, branches, and uniform cuts. The photo was taken at a medical school very early in the war.

This group photo taken in 1916 of medics and soldiers in other branches of service displays a wide variety of materials used in the making of gymnastiorki (field blouses). In addition to the wide variety of materials displayed are also the models and materials of gymnastiorki used during different seasons.

This photo was taken at a studio in Moscow in 1916. The shoulder boards (pogoni) indicate the soldier is from the Grand Duchess/Princess Olga Regiment. The braided piping bordering his pogoni was typical for volunteers. The badge worn on his right side is from the Russian Red Cross. The Grand Duchess/Princess Olga Alexandrova Romanova, a sibling of the Czar, became a nurse and worked with the wounded during the First World War.

This medic wears a shinel, or brownish gray overcoat, made of a heavy grade of wool. His armband is made of oilcloth, hence its shiny and slick appearance. His Red Cross cockade on his hat is made of aluminum. Riga, Latvia (Baltic State/Country), 1916

Although not officially nor medically proven, tree climbing with the nurses seems to speed the recovery of the wounded soldiers as seen in this photo. The soldier standing on the limb (left), who has his left hand holding a nurse and his right holding on to a branch, wears a cavalry regimental badge. Moscow 1915.

This photo was taken on the coast of Estonia (Baltic State/Country) in 1917. The nurses wear clothing issued to them by the Red Cross. The armband of the nurse sitting on the rail (right) reveals an issue ink stamp. All wear a red and white enamel Red Cross brooch.

This studio photo was taken in 1916 in Tallinn, Estonia (Baltic State/Country). The nurse stands behind an officer in a Siberian regiment who is wearing a classic heavy wool officer tunic (kitel) and trousers. His visor hat has the stiff construction look preferred by officers. The stiff construction look was obtained by using starch, cardboard, or wire.

A studio photo taken in St. Petersburg in 1915. Both soldiers wear issue shineli—the term given for brownish gray wool overcoats—as well as issue papahi (astrakhan or winter wool fleece cap). The differences in the color of collar patches can be seen, in addition to their painted shoulder boards.

A studio photo of a nurse and some of her patients taken in 1915. This photo displays a variety of styles—the way a furashka (field cap) could be worn, as well as the various cuts and modifications that could be made to a gymnastiorka (field blouse). The soldier in the center, with the vertical cloth stripe on his gymnastiorka and his lighter colored leather belt, indicates he is from a Guards Regiment. Leather belts were also painted white or other colors according to Regimental colors.

This photo was taken in 1917. This soldier wears a cotton gymnastiorka (field blouse) with wool shoulder boards (pogoni). The Red Cross is made of a different grade of wool and has been stitched to the shoulder boards.

This cabinet portrait was taken in 1916. The medic appears to be ready for the harsh demands of a Russian winter. He wears a papaha (astrakhan or winter fur/fleece cap) made of thick fur, which almost buries his cockade. Slightly visible are his Red Cross shoulder boards (pogoni) made from the same brownish gray wool as his overcoat, or shinel.

A studio photo taken in 1915 in Tallinn, Estonia (Baltic State/Country). These four medics wear issue gymnastiorki which they have belted. Each belt worn by the medics is a different model. The soldier's black papaha is typical of the type worn by soldiers in Siberian Regiments or Cossacks. The soldier sitting next to him wears an issue papaha.

This studio photo was taken in Tallinn, Estonia (Baltic State/Country). The medic wears an oversized heavy cotton gymnastiorka with wool shoulder boards. The Red Crosses have been painted on the shoulder boards. He wears an aluminum Red Cross cockade on his furashka (visor cap).

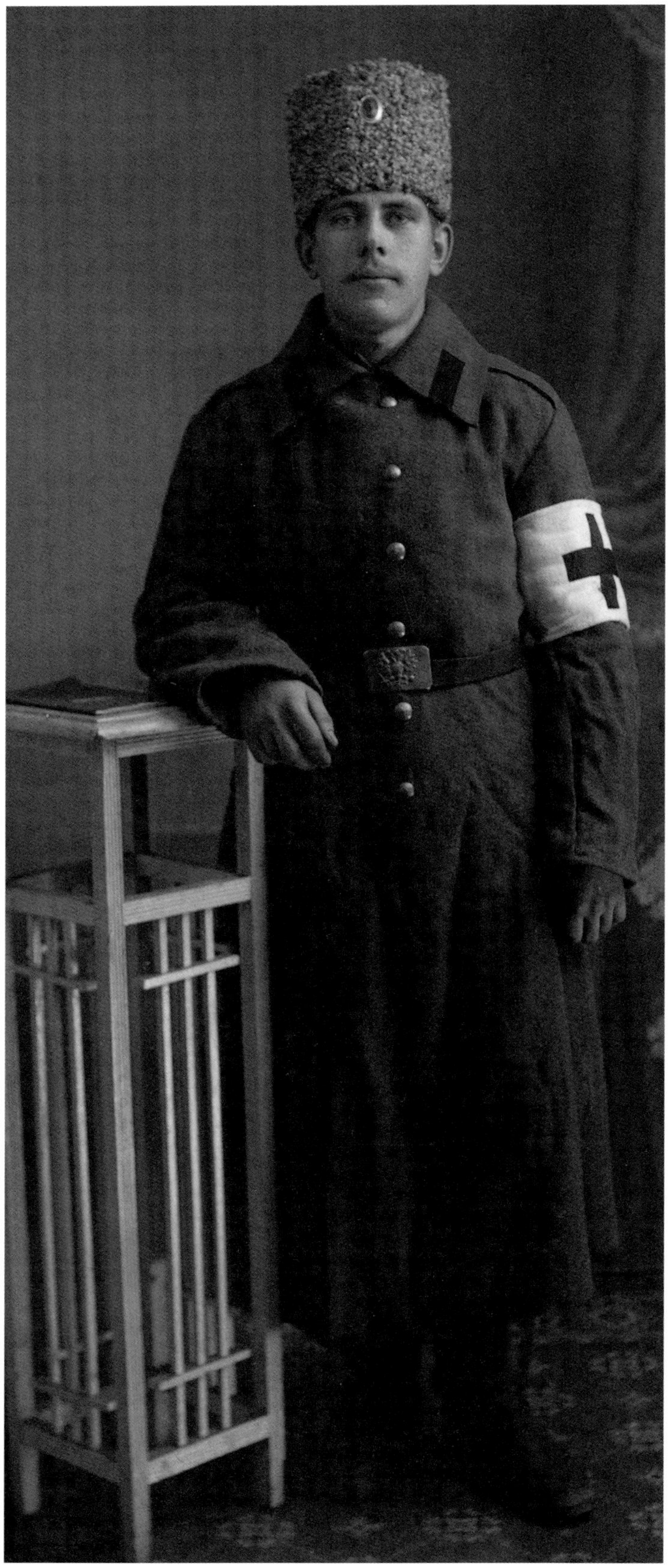

Most papahi (astrakhan or winter fleece/fur caps) were crushable, with sides that unhooked and folded down for protection in harsh weather. However, there were also stiff construction papahi as well, which had more of a cylindrical shape, such as the one this medic is wearing. These stiff construction papahi had cardboard or hardened leather backing the fleece, thus making it more rigid, but not as functional or practical as the crushable papaha. Both the crushable and the stiff papahi were either issued at a depot or could be privately purchased.

This studio photo taken in Riga, Latvia (Baltic State/Country), in 1916 displays the subtle variations which existed in issued gymnastiorki, and in the marking of wool shoulder boards (pogoni). For example, on the shoulder boards of the soldier on the left the red cross has been painted on, whereas the red cross on the other soldiers' shoulder boards consists of two pieces of wool crossed and then stitched on. Examples of the subtle variations in the gymnastiorki are seen in the different buttons used, as well as the varying shades of material caused by different dyeing processes.

This medic appears to be ready for a harsh winter at the front. His sherst (wool) bashlik (cowl or hood), which provided extra protection against harsh weather conditions, has been secured by his shoulder boards (pogoni) and waist belt. He has the strap from his medical bag flung over his left shoulder, and the straps from his canteen flung over his right. Straps were made of either leather (usually pigskin) or woven cloth, depending upon availability of material. His aluminum canteen has a greenish brown wool cover, which was normally stitched on, however, wool covers that snapped over the canteen were also used. The drinking cup is held in place by leather straps, which were stitched to the leather and then buttoned to an aluminum knob.

This photo was taken at a hospital near Moscow in 1914. These are a few of the many wounded to come from Russia as the war progressed.

A group photo of soldiers and their nurses at a hospital near the southern front in 1916.

This group of medics is carefully removing a soldier from a stretcher carried by horses from the front.

A field hospital on the Front sjéwerny (Northern front). Three of the soldiers seen here wear Latvian Riflemen Badges.

This is an official photo taken from a series produced in 1914 to fund the War. The Cyrillic inscription reads, "From the Theatre of War. The Regiment of the Red Cross."

Chapter Three

General Infantry (All Ranks)

This frontovik (frontline soldier) wears an issued wool furashka (visor cap) and gymnastiorka (field blouse). He has his rolled overcoat, or blanket, as well as ais bandolier flung over his left shoulder. Over his right shoulder he has flung his wool covered aluminum canteen and bread bag, or gasmask bag. He is armed with an M1891 Mosin-Nagant rifle, the ammunition for which he carries in the two leather ammo pouches and bandolier. 1914.

This officer, who is diligently studying a battle map, wears a privately tailored sherst (wool) gymnastiorka (field blouse) with gold stitched pogoni (shoulder boards), 1915.

This is a fantastic studio collage photo that was produced in a standard postcard (4 x 6 inch) size! This is an invaluable resource, as it reveals every angle of the gymnastiorka (field blouse) and furashka (visor hat). 1915.

This cabinet portrait was taken in 1914. Government officials, cadets, and officers preferred the dark green wool overcoat worn by this soldier. The double-headed Romanov eagle collar insignia is gilded and fastened to his velvet collar stripe by either a pin or fastened with a disk, which screwed on the back of the insignia. The cockade on his greenish brown heavy wool visor hat was also preferred by government officials, cadets, and officers.

This NCO is from the 25th Siberian Rifle Regiment. He wears a privately tailored gymnastiorka (field blouse). This photo also reveals the detail and construction of his belt. 1916.

The soldier in this studio photo wears an issue gymnastiorka (field blouse) made of cotton and an issue furashka (visor hat) made of wool. The decoration he wears is a Romanov commemorative medal: the colors of the ribbon are red (left) and the colors of the Romanov dynasty orange and black (right). 1915.

The soldier in this cabinet portrait has his issued gymnastiorka (field blouse) belted with a cloth web belt. His privately made sapogi (boots), which fit very high up his legs, provide protection from harsh weather conditions. Southern Russia, 1915.

This photo was taken in southern Russia in 1915. The soldier sitting on the left wears a gymnastiorka made of khlopok (cotton). The NCO sitting in the middle wears a shinel (brownish gray wool overcoat). The soldier sitting on the right wears a gymnastiorka made of belyo (linen). The two soldiers standing in the background wear privately tailored wool gymnastiorki (field blouses). Normally flowers were given to troops who were heading to the front.

This studio photo was taken in Tallinn, Estonia (Baltic State/Country), in 1915. The soldier wears a stiffened visor cap, and a privately made coarse brown tweed tunic with exterior pleated pockets and a metal number "3" pinned to his collar.

This photo was taken in a Moscow studio in 1916. The cockade on the soldier's furashka (visor cap) has been subdued or camouflaged by sewing a piece of wool over it. The three stripes on his shoulder boards, which are made of coarser wool than the gymnastiorka, indicate he is an NCO. His regiment numbers are faintly visible on his pogoni (shoulder boards).

This is a soldier of enlisted rank from the No.429 Rishski Infantry Regiment as indicated by the numbers painted on his wool pogoni (shoulder boards). His issued gymnastiorka (field blouse) is made of cotton and his issued furashka (visor cap) is wool. His wristwatch is actually a pocket watch encased in leather. The No. 2 Latvian, No. 3 Border Patrol and No.11 Dragoon Regiments were also named Rishski. Moscow 1915

These two NCOs are from the No. 113 Starorusski Infantry Regiment, as their shoulder board (pogoni) markings indicate. They both wear privately made gymnastiorki (field blouses) and stiffened furashki (visor caps). Minsk 1915.

Left: This soldier from No. 198 Alexandro-Newski Infantry Regiment is wearing a privately tailored tunic and visor cap based on the M1910. The grip and guard on his saber have been customized. 1915. Right: The soldier standing on the right in this 1915 vintage studio photo has been awarded the St. George Cross (Svjatoi Georggi Orden) for valor. The cloth lightning bolts stitched to his left sleeve indicate he is from a signal battalion. Both soldiers have Latvian Riflemen Badges fastened to the left button flap of their gymnastiorki.

The soldiers seen here have a fresh from the front and then to a photo studio look. The light-colored stripes on the cuff and chest of their issued gymnastiorki (field blouses), as well as the light colored belt the soldier on the right is wearing, indicate these soldiers are possibly from a Guards Regiment. 1915.

This is a cabinet portrait taken in 1917. The NCO wears a coarse brownish gray wool overcoat (shinel) and carries a saber with sword knot. The cylindrical leather pouch on his left leather strap is made to hold a whistle.

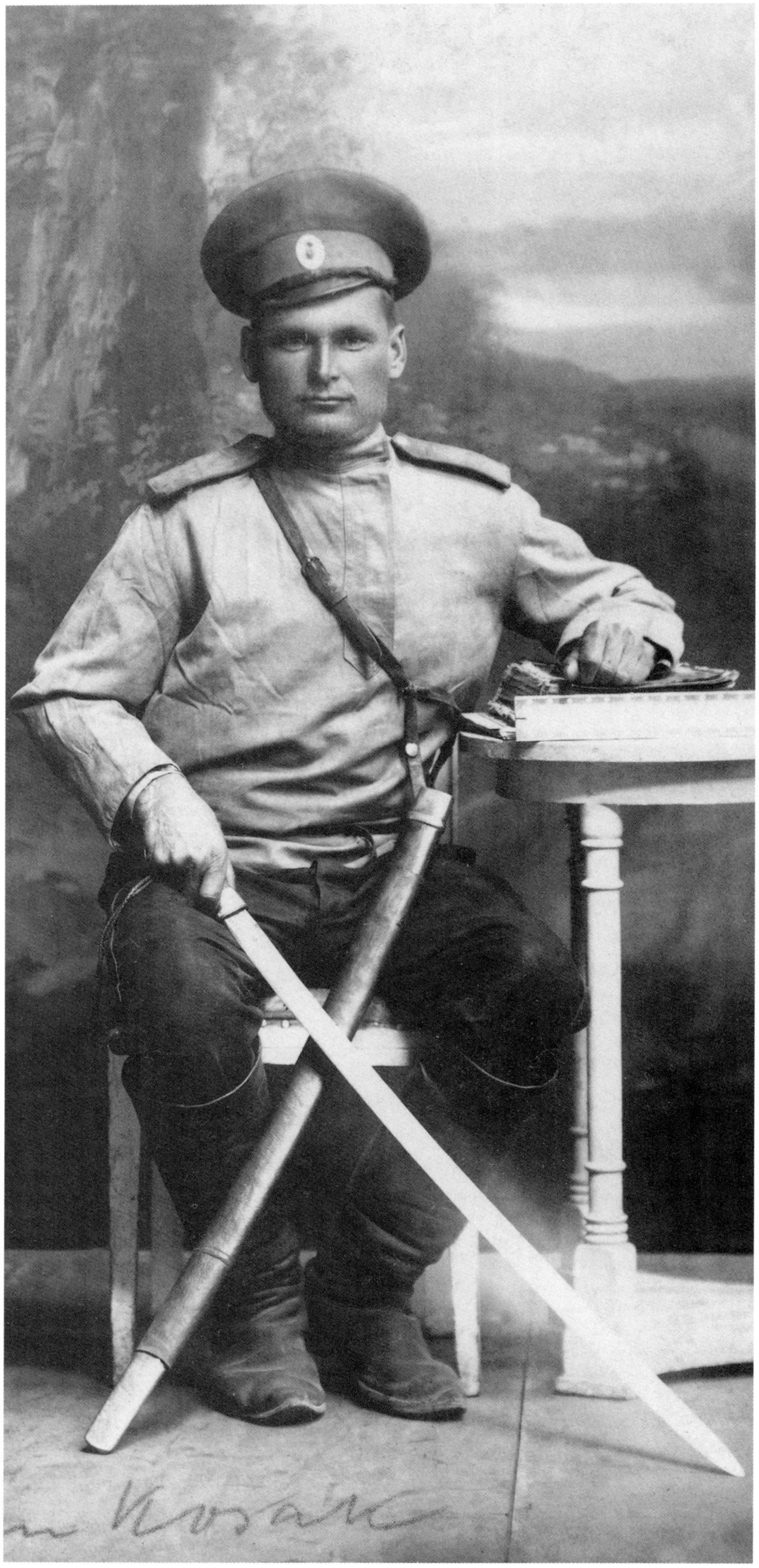

This enlisted rank soldier, who is proudly displaying his shaska (Cossack saber), wears a cotton gymnastiorka (field blouse) and a stiffened furashka (visor cap). Furashki were stiffened with either starch, cardboard, or wire. This photo was taken in a studio in St. Petersburg in 1915.

The two soldiers holding the bike handles in this cabinet portrait wear privately tailored gymnastiorki. Each is armed with a bebout (long curved knife), which was an edged weapon preferred by artillerists and forward scouts.

This photo was taken in a studio in Warsaw, Poland. These soldiers are from the No. 48 Dnjeprowski Infantry Regiment and wear the pre- to early-war white cotton gymnastiorki (field blouses) and sharovari (dark green wool pants). This style of gymnastiorki and sharovari were abandoned as the war progressed.

This photo was taken in a studio in Moscow in 1916. These soldiers wear a classic, roughly cut brownish gray overcoat (shineli) with blank shoulder boards (pogoni) that is depot issued. Their furashki and belts are issue, as well. Belts normally were made of pigskin, and the belt buckles with the Romanov double-headed eagle motifs were made of brass.

This NCO is from the No. 111 Donskoi Infantry Regiment. His furashka (visor cap) is made of brown wool and has a stiffened look. He wears a privately tailored greenish brown wool gymnastiorka (field blouse) with two exterior pleated breast pockets. 1917.

This cabinet portrait was taken in 1915 and displays a wide variety of privately tailored wool gymnastiorki (field blouses) worn by NCOs during this period. The soldier standing in the center with the dark wool stripe sewn next to his buttons is possibly from a Guard Regiment.

This photo offers a glimpse of industry during the Czarist period. The backward and inefficient industry caused many of the problems for the armed forces experienced during the First World War, such as not being able to produce enough ammunition, and not being able to properly outfit troops because of material shortages.

This group photo taken near Moscow in 1916 shows a wide variety of uniform models. Seated in the front row center is the Regimental Priest. The officer seated on the left of the Regimental Priest has been awarded the St. George Cross for valor. The soldier seated to the right, with his hands folded over his M1881 officer's saber, wears an Order of Vladimir neck decoration.

This photo was taken at a studio in Estonia (Baltic State/Country) in 1915. The NCO wears a privately tailored brown tweed gymnastoirka (field blouse). The furashka (visor cap) he wears appears to be issue.

The soldiers in this studio photo taken in 1915 wear issued gymnastiorki (field blouses) and furashki (visor caps). Both carry the M1881 saber with a leather sword knot. The spurs on the boots of the soldier on the left indicate he is from a mounted regiment.

The two soldiers in this 1917 vintage studio photo have Latvian Riflemen badges fastened to their privately tailored gymnastiorki (field blouses). Both have their hands resting next to an Adrian style steel helmet with a Romanov doubled headed eagle badge fastened to it. At their feet are an artillery round and a rolled wool overcoat (shinel).

The NCO in this studio photo wears a heavy wool overcoat (shinel) with wool shoulder boards (pogoni) bearing metal crossed cannon insignia, indicating he is from an artillery unit. He has a metal cockade with black and orange roundels fastened to his mink ushanka, which is a winter cap with earflaps that fasten together atop the head.

This officer wears a greenish brown single-breasted tunic made of a heavy grade of wool. In addition, he wears a school/academy badge on his right breast pocket. Wearing badges from cavalry or cadet schools/academies was popular with NCO and officers throughout the course of the war. Badges were exquisitely crafted by various manufacturers and varied in shape and size. Most badges were gilded, enameled, or both.

This officer wears a stiffened greenish brown wool visor cap with a porcelain cockade and a gilded Romanov double-headed eagle. His tunic is double breasted and made of a heavy grade of greenish brown wool. The lanyard around his neck is attached to a 7.62mm M1895 Nagant seven round revolver. Also visible is his saber and sword knot.

This cabinet portrait was taken in St. Petersburg. The soldier on the left, gripping his M1881 saber, wears a visor cap made of a heavy grade of greenish brown wool with a porcelain cockade. The seated soldier smoking a cigarette wears a summer weight visor cap with porcelain cockade and a white tunic.

Four of the five soldiers in this photo wear three-quarter length wool tunics—a style preferred by Cossacks—and each is armed with a shaska (Cossack saber).

This NCO is from the No. 132 Benderski Infantry Regiment, as the metal number pinned to his pogoni indicates. He wears a visor cap made of a heavy grade of greenish brown wool with a porcelain cockade stitched to the band. His greenish brown wool tunic is privately tailored, and the leather strap around the outside of his left cuff is for a wristwatch. This photo was taken as a souvenir cabinet portrait in Riga, Latvia (Baltic State/Country), 1915.

These two enlisted rank soldiers wear issued wool overcoats (shineil) with cloth bandoliers flung over their left shoulders. Both are armed with Japanese manufactured Arisaka rifles and bayonets.

Left: This cabinet portrait was taken in St. Petersburg in 1916. The seated NCO wears a classic greenish brown wool tunic with matching trousers and visor cap. The soldier standing is intriguing. He wears an issued sherst (wool) gymnastiorka (field blouse) with shoulder boards made of different color wool that bear no rank or regiment markings. His stiffened visor cap is made of black wool with a black velvet band. Stitched to the black velvet band is an enlisted rank cockade with a gilded double-headed Romanov eagle above it. He has what appears to be a silver or gilded badge from a Guard or cavalry regiment pinned to his gymnastiorka, which he has belted with a pigskin leather belt and Grenadier's brass belt buckle. He also wears dark wool trousers, or sharovari. Right: This enlisted rank soldier wears an issued cotton gymnastiorka (field blouse) and furashka (visor cap), as well as dark green wool trousers, or sharovari. He has the woven cloth strap of his wool covered aluminum canteen with cork stopper flung over his right shoulder. The woven cloth strap is held in place by three small straps of leather stitched to the wool cover around the canteen. There were various materials used in making canteens, such as glass, wood, and aluminum. Those made of aluminum bear a manufacturer's mark and a production date around the neck of the canteen. Minsk, 1915.

The rugged looking officer in this 1916 vintage photo wears a privately tailored wool tunic with stiffened shoulder boards (pogoni) bearing a metal number "3." He has secured the leather chinstrap on his wool visor cap with a rosette cockade.

This officer wears red enamel and gold or gilded Star of the Order of St. Stanislaus with swords pinned to his privately tailored greenish brown tunic. The Order of St. Stanislaus dates from the 1700s and is of Polish origin, having been founded by King Stanislaus Augustus, who was pro-Russian. The Order was abolished and reinstated numerous times since its founding. This photo of the officer and his wife was taken on August 15, 1915.

The soldier in this photo taken in 1915 captures the rugged simplicity of the Russian soldier in the First World War. The simple cut and material of his gymnastiorka, which is most likely homemade, give the soldier a look of having come right from the countryside to the battlefield.

The officer in this studio photo wears a privately tailored wool tunic (kitel) with gold stitched shoulder boards (pogoni). Hanging on his left side is a dagger/dirk with an ivory handle (kortik). Normally, the kortik was reserved for parades or dress, but for a decadent appearance, an officer could wear one on the battlefield. Officers and NCOs in all branches of the armed forces wore a kortik, particularly those in Air and Naval service branches.

This studio photo was taken in St. Petersburg in 1914. The soldier on the left wears a privately tailored gymnastiorka (field blouse) made of greenish brown wool. The soldier on the right wears a pre- to early-war white cotton gymnastiorka. Both soldiers wear dark green wool trousers known as sharovari. The spurs on each soldier's boots indicate they are from a mounted regiment. Their furashki are wool with a leather chinstrap. This style of furashka was preferred by those soldiers serving in mounted regiments, but was also worn by those serving in the infantry, as well. Both soldiers display front and side views of the blade of the M1881 saber.

These soldiers are from the No. 270 Gatschinski Infantry Regiment, as indicated by the numbers painted on their shoulder boards. All wear issued wool gymnastoirka (field blouses). The soldier on the left wears a wool pillbox shaped cap, or pilotka. Pilotaka were worn in the field just the like the furashka (visor cap). The Cyrillic inscription reads "In Memory of My Military Service." Moscow, 1915.

This soldier's leather visor cap, tunic, and boots appear very weathered and well worn. Due to regular exposure to the elements, motorists and aviators preferred leather gear. It is interesting to note that his pogoni (shoulder boards) bear no numbers or insignia, and appear to be made of wool. This photo is dated 12 IV, 1916.

These four NCOs pause for a photo to demonstrate not only their ability as soldiers, but also their ability as beekeepers. Russian soldiers used natural substances like honey for medicinal purposes. In addition to honey, garlic was also used for medicinal purposes. 1915.

This group of soldiers pauses briefly from their card playing, smoking, and letter writing for the photographer to snap a photo. This photo displays not only a group of soldiers relaxing and enjoying comradeship, but also a wide variety of khlopok (cotton), belyo (linen), and sherstjanaja (wool) gymnastiorki (field blouses). The field equipment in the center consists of backpacks, blankets, and two copper mess kits. The NCO standing in the center with a cigarette between his fingers and his thumbs tucked into his belt has been awarded the St. George's Cross, as indicated by the orange and black ribbon sewn diagonally between the buttons of his gymnastiorka. Minsk, 1915.

This studio photo was taken in Kiev in 1916. These soldiers wear brownish gray wool (shineli) overcoats made of a heavy grade of wool. Their wool visor caps have been stiffened using either starch, wire, or cardboard. The stripes on their sleeves and shoulder boards indicate their rank.

These two soldiers wear issued papahi (astrakhan or fleece/fur winter caps) and shineli (wool overcoats). The soldier on the right wears a brass belt buckle bearing a Romanov double-headed eagle with crossed cannons motif, which artillerists preferred. Both are armed with M1891 Mosin-Nagant rifles. February 1915.

This group photo shows soldiers from the No. 27 Witebski Infantry Regiment, as well as a wide variety of materials and cuts used in gymnastiorka and wool overcoats. This photo was taken outside Riga, Latvia (Baltic State/Country), in 1915.

This group of NCOs from the No. 3 Kursemski Latvian Rifles relax on the grass in a field in Latvia to read copies of a local newspaper and enjoy the company of one of the local ladies in 1916.

Above: This group of soldiers wearing furashki (visor caps) and gymnastiorki (field blouses) appear ready to head to the front! They carry Koumant-Zelinski gasmasks and are armed with Japanese manufactured Arisaka rifles and bayonets. The ammunition for their rifles is carried in either cloth bandoliers or leather ammo pouches. 1916.

Right: The soldier in this 1915 vintage studio photo is armed with an M1891 Mosin-Nagant rifle, the ammunition for which he carries in his cloth bandolier and leather ammo pouches. He has a general-purpose pouch flung over his right shoulder.

The group of soldiers in this 1916 studio photo wear their khlopok (cotton) gymnastiorki (field blouses) belted. The soldier standing on the left wears a pre- to early-war wool forage cap. The other three wear wool visor caps that they have stiffened with either starch, wire, or cardboard. The two soldiers wearing visor caps made of light greenish brown colored wool have covered their cockades using the same light color wool. The soldier seated on the right wears wool shoulder boards with white piping and a pocket watch that he has converted to a wristwatch.

The two NCOs in this studio photo wear issued wool overcoats (shineli) with collar patches and shoulder boards (pogoni) made of a different color wool. The NCO on the left has taken his Nagant revolver out of its holster. Both are armed with M1881 sabers.

These three soldiers of enlisted rank wear issued sherstjanaja (wool) gymnastiorki (field blouses) that they have belted with pigskin leather belts with brass buckles. All three wear issued wool pillbox shaped forage caps with metal cockades. The roundels on their cockades are painted orange and black. 1915.

Left: The frontovik (frontline soldier) in this photo is armed with an M1891 Mosin Nagant rifle, the ammunition for which he carries in two leather ammo pouches. He has secured his backpack by tucking the cloth straps under his shoulder boards (pogoni). Also visible in this photo is the wood handle of his shovel/entrenching tool. Right: These soldiers wear oversized, roughly cut, brownish gray wool winter overcoats (shineli) and stiffened furashki (visor caps) with a cockade that helps to hold their privately purchased goggles in place. The soldier on the right is armed with a bebout (long curved knife—an edged weapon preferred by artillerists and scouts), as well as a holstered Nagant revolver with a cloth cord lanyard.

The officer in this cabinet portrait taken in 1916 wears a privately tailored greenish brown sherst (wool) gymnastoirka with two breast pockets. The cylindrical leather pouch sewn to his leather straps is for a whistle. He carries a customized saber with a sword knot.

The four soldiers in this 1916 vintage studio photo wear issued brownish gray wool winter overcoats (shineli) and furashki (visor caps), to which they have fastened Militia Crosses. Militia Crosses were worn by volunteers, reservists, and National guardsmen. All four are armed with Berdan rifles and bayonets.

Southwest Front, 1916.

These soldiers examine an observation instrument at a camp in Southern Russia in 1914. The soldier holding the observation instrument wears a pre- to early-war gymnastiorka.

Left: The bearded soldier seated on the left wears a privately tailored sherst (wool) gymnastoirka (field blouse), and a visor cap that has been stiffened with either starch, cardboard, or wire. The two other soldiers wear issued khlopok (cotton) gymnastoirka and issued sherst furashka (visor cap). This studio photo was taken in 1916. Right: This officer from the No. 239 Konstaninogradski Infantry Regiment wears a privately tailored overcoat and visor cap. His visor cap has been stiffened with either wire or cardboard. His saber is concealed by his overcoat. 1916.

Left: This NCO is from the No. 24 Simbirski Infantry Regiment. He wears a privately tailored, double pocketed sherst (wool) gymnastiorka (field blouse). In his right he clutches his M1881 saber. The brass fittings on the scabbard are for holding a 17-inch long M1891 Nagant bayonet. 1916. Right: The NCO seated in this studio portrait taken in 1915 wears a privately tailored sherst (wool) gymnastoirka (field blouse) that has two exterior pleated pockets with a watch chain suspended between them. He wears a very unusual pair of sapogi (boots) that were custom made to meet the demands of the trenches.

This group of soldiers is from the No. 430 Walkski Infantry Regiment, as their wool shoulder boards indicate. The officer sitting in the center with his arms folded wears an enameled Order of St. Anne (Svjatoi Anny Orden) with swords around his neck. The Duke of Holstein-Gottorp, Karl Frederick, founded the order of St. Anne in 1735. He founded it to honor his wife Anna Petrovna, who was the daughter of Peter the Great. It was the first foreign order for merit to be adopted by Russia.

The group of soldiers in this studio photo taken in Riga, Latvia (Baltic State/Country), in 1915 is from a Latvian Rifle Battalion. The round badges worn by these Latvian Riflemen bear the inscription LSB. Although serving in the Russian Armed Forces, Latvians were commanded by Latvian officers and fought largely in their own country.

The two soldiers in this studio photo are from a Latvian Rifle Battalion. The soldier seated on the left wears an issued sherst gymnastiorka, which he has belted with a single prong buckle pigskin belt, and an issued sherst furashka (visor cap). Pinned to the pocket flap of the left breast pocket of his gymnastiorka is a metal Latvian Rifleman Badge bearing the letters LSB. His footwear consists of a pair of leather hob-nailed, lace-up ankle boots, as well as a pair of leather gaiters. The soldier standing on the right also wears an issued gymnastiorka with a Latvian Rifleman Badge pinned below the pocket flap of his left breast pocket. Above the lower button on his gymnastiorka he has sewn a rather faded black and orange striped ribbon, indicating he has been decorated with the St. George Cross for valor. He has camouflaged the cockade on his furashka (visor cap) by sewing a piece of wool over it. His footwear consists of leather hob-nailed lace up ankle boots, the tops of which he has covered with his wool puttees. Riga, Latvia (Baltic State/Country), 1916.

The NCO seated in this studio photo grasping his M1881 saber with leather sword wears a privately tailored brownish green tunic made of a heavy grade of wool. The buttons on his tunic are brass with a Romanov double-headed eagle motif. Moscow, 1916.

The soldier in this studio photo taken in 1916 wears a khlopok (cotton) gymnastiorka (field blouse) with wool pogoni (shoulder boards). The cloth stripe running the length of his button was a style characteristic of those soldiers serving in Guard units.

Left: Both soldiers in this studio photo taken in 1915 wear issued wool furashka (visor cap) and brownish gray winter overcoats made of a heavy grade of wool (shinel). They are holding Japanese manufactured Arisaka rifles. The Russian Armed Forces imported many arms from more industrialized nations. However, these Arisakas were most likely captured in the Russo-Japanese War of 1904. Right: The soldier in this studio photo taken in 1915 wears an issued sherst (wool) furashka (visor cap) that has been stiffened with either wire or cardboard. Women were allowed to serve in the Russian Armed Forces in the First World War.

Left: This photo was taken in the Russian countryside. The officer in the center, with his left hand resting on his M1881 saber, is from a Life Guard Regiment, as indicated by his shoulder boards. He has covered the metal cockade on his white cotton visor cap. His double-breasted tunic is made of a heavy grade of greenish brown wool, and he wears dark green wool trousers known as sharovari. The two NCOs wear white khlopok (cotton) gymnastiorka (field blouse) and sharovari. They have their gymnastiorki belted with a pigskin leather, brass buckled belt. The raised motif on their brass buckles is that of a flaming cannon ball, indicating these soldiers are Grenadiers. Right: The soldier in this 1916 vintage studio has the St. George Cross (Svjatoi Georggi Orden) for valor pinned to his winter overcoat (shinel). In addition, he has cloth insignia depicting two interlocking electric bolts stitched on his left sleeve, which indicate he is from a telegraph/telephone unit.

This studio photo was taken in Riga, Latvia (Baltic State/Country), in 1915. The officer in the center wears a privately tailored tunic with two pleated exterior breast pockets. Pinned to his left button flap is a Latvian Rifleman Badge. His visor cap has been stiffened with either starch, cardboard, or wire. The soldier of enlisted rank smoking a cigarette wears a privately tailored, double-pocketed gymnastiorka made of a heavy grade of greenish brown wool (sherst). He has also stiffened his visor cap, and has pinned a Latvian Rifleman Badge to his left button flap. The soldier on the right has given his visor cap a crushed look. The three are wearing patriotic ribbons.

This group of soldiers are from various ranks and wear a variety of uniform styles. The two soldiers on the ground, as well as the one standing on the right with his left hand on his saber, wear hooded trench coats.

These officers and NCOs are seated on the edge of a shell hole. The officer seated in the center wears an Adrian style steel helmet with a Romanov double-headed eagle badge fastened to the front. He carries a Koumant-Zelinski Model gasmask, as do his two comrades seated on his left and right side.

This group of soldiers are clad in various styles of furashki (visor caps) and gymnastiorki (field blouses). In addition, many have Latvian Rifleman badges, or the St. George Cross (Svjatoi Georggi Orden) for valor fastened to their gymnastiorki. 1915.

These soldiers are visiting with their families before they leave for the front, 1915.

Left: The officer in this studio photo wears a wool tunic (kitel) with stiff gold stitched shoulder boards (pogoni). He is armed with an intricately detailed officer's saber and a holstered 7.62 mm caliber, seven round Nagant revolver. Tallinn, Estonia (Baltic State/Country), 1916.

Below: The three soldiers in this studio wear wool furashki (visor caps) with Militia Crosses fastened above their cockades. Militia Crosses were worn by volunteers, reservists, and national guardsmen. The soldier standing on the right wears a unique striped gymnastiorka (field blouse), 1915.

Left: The NCO in this 1915 vintage studio photo wears a wool overcoat (shinel) with a black and orange ribbon stitched to his button flap, indicating he has been awarded the St. George Cross (Svjatoi Georggi Orden) for valor. He is armed with an M1891 bayonet for the Mosin-Nagant rifle. Right: The two soldiers in this studio photo wear privately tailored, double breast-pocketed wool gymnastiorki (field blouses) and are armed with M1881 sabers. The soldier seated on the left has a black and orange striped ribbon stitched between the buttons on his gymnastiorka (field blouse), indicating he has been awarded the St. George Cross (Svjatoi Georggi Orden) for valor. 1916.

The soldier seated on the left wears a privately tailored greenish brown wool gymnastiorka. The other three soldiers wear double-breasted dark green wool tunics. This cabinet portrait was taken in 1914.

Left: The two mustached soldiers in this studio photo have Latvian Riflemen badges fastened to their sherstjanaja (wool) gymnastiorki (field blouses). Both wear French Adrian style steel helmets with Romanov double-headed eagle badges fastened to the front. Riga, Latvia (Baltic State/Country), 1916. Right: This NCO, proudly clutching his M1881 saber, wears a brownish gray wool winter overcoat which he has belted. Moscow, 1915.

Left: The mustached officer in this studio photo wears a double-breasted gray overcoat made of a heavy grade of wool. The buttons on his overcoat are brass with a raised Romanov double-headed eagle motif. His visor cap has been stiffened with either starch, cardboard, or wire. St. Petersburg, 1915. Right: A soldier from the 266 Porjetschenski Infantry Regiment. He has secured his leather chinstrap on his furashka (visor cap) with his oval cockade.

The soldier sitting on the rocks wears a double breast-pocketed privately tailored wool gymnastiorka (field blouse) with woolen shoulder boards bearing telegraph/telephone operator insignia. The two NCOs standing on either side also wear double breast-pocketed, privately tailored wool gymnastiorka. The NCO on the right has been awarded the St. George Cross for valor.

The NCO on the left wears a privately tailored, greenish brown sherst gymnastiorka with dark green wool trousers (sharovari). The NCO on the right wears a gymnastiorka made of dark green wool that he had privately tailored, and sharovari. The lanyards around their neck most likely attach to their 7.62 mm caliber M1895 Nagant seven round pistols, which they have chosen to conceal. However, both NCOs have decided to proudly display the blades of their M1881 sabers. 1916.

The soldier seated in this studio photo is from the No. 36 Orlowski Infantry Regiment, as the metal numbers on his stiffened shoulder boards indicate. August 25, 1916.

The three soldiers in this pre- to early-war vintage photo wear double-breasted dark green wool tunics and carry M1881 sabers. Two of the soldiers have ammunition belts around their waists. In addition, the soldier on the left wears a marksmen badge.

Left: This soldier has a military school badge fastened, privately tailored wool gymnastiorka. Front sjéwerny (Northern front), 1915. Right: The NCO on the right in this studio photo wears a privately tailored double breast-pocketed gymnastiorka (field blouse) with wool pogoni (shoulder boards) outlined in braided cloth piping. He has a Latvian Riflemen badge fastened to the left button flap on his gymnastiorka. The soldier on the left wears a khlopok (cotton) gymnastiorka with wool pogoni. He has a Militia Cross fastened above the cockade on his furashka (visor cap).

The mounted officer wears a khlopok (cotton) gymnastiorka with gold stitched pogoni (shoulder boards). The two enlisted rank soldiers wear cotton gymnastiorki (field blouses) with wool pogoni. Both are armed with M1891 Mosin-Nagant rifles, the ammunition for which they carry in their cloth bandoliers and leather ammo pouches.

These two enlisted rank soldiers are in full service dress and ready for the front. Their furashki (visor caps), gymnastiorki (field blouses), sapogi (boots), and trousers appear entirely depot issued. They have rolled their wool blankets or overcoats, flung them over their left shoulders, and tucked the ends in their copper mess tins, or krushki. They both are holding M1891 Mosin-Nagant rifles with bayonets fixed, and wear both cloth bandoliers and leather ammo pouches, which hold 7.62mm caliber rounds. On the back of this postcard-size photo is the date August 1914.

This soldiers in this 1917 vintage photo are clad in winter overcoats (shineli), papahi (astrakhan or fleece/fur winter caps), and Adrian style steel helmets. They are armed with Japanese manufactured Arisaka rifles and bayonets.

This group of recruits, volunteers, and national guardsmen are clad in military and civilian clothing and are armed with M1891 Mosin-Nagant rifles and bayonets. Many wear Militia Crosses in addition to cockades on their headdress.

Left: The mustached officer in this studio photo wears a privately tailored greenish brown wool tunic with concealed buttons and dark green wool trousers, or sharovari. His wool visor cap with leather chinstrap has been stiffened, most likely with wire. St. Petersburg, 1915. Right: This officer wears a privately tailored gymnastiorka with two pleated exterior breast pockets and made from a heavy grade of greenish brown wool. He carries a saber with sword knot. 1916.

The soldier standing on the left wears a wrinkled khlopok (cotton) gymnastoirka that he has belted with a single-prong buckle leather belt. The soldier seated on the right wears a privately tailored sherst (wool) gymnastiorka with two pleated exterior breast pockets. Both soldiers wear wool visor caps with leather chinstraps. 1916.

These soldiers in this 1915 photo wear issued gymnastiorki and furashki. The mustached soldier seated on the left has a St. George Cross (Svjatoi Georggi Orden) for valor and a Romanov medal pinned to his gymnastiorka.

This bicyclist wears a privately tailored, double breast pocketed khlopok (cotton) gymnastiorka, which he has belted with a leather belt with a two-prong buckle. Riga, Latvia (Baltic State/Country), 1915.

Living conditions on the front, 1915.

The soldier seated in this photo wears an issued khlopok gymnastiorka, which he has belted. He has his wool-covered canteen slung over his right shoulder. The regimental number "146" is painted on his wool shoulder boards. Moscow 1915.

The group of soldiers in this pre- to early-war vintage photo wear white cotton gymnastiorki and furashki. In addition, all wear dark green wool trousers (sharovari) and various cuts of pre- to early-war tunics and shineli (wool overcoats).

The soldiers in this 1915 vintage photo exhibit a variety of shineli and furashki. Many of these soldiers have leather ammo pouches fastened to their waist belts.

The NCO standing on the left wears a privately tailored sherst (wool) gymnastiorka (field blouse), which he has belted. Pinned to his gymnastiorka are two Romanov medals, a cavalry or cadet school badge, and an enameled cross badge. The soldier standing on the right wears a khlopok (cotton) gymnastiorka. Hanging from his belt is an Austrian manufactured M1895 bayonet. 1915.

Above: This soldier, standing in a forest on the northern front, wears a papaha (astrakhan or fleece/fur winter cap) and a heavy wool winter overcoat (shinel). He is armed with a Japanese manufactured Arisaka rifle and bayonet.

Right: The soldier in this studio photo wears a privately tailored gymnastiorka (field blouse) and dark green wool trousers known as sharovari. He is armed with a Berdan rifle and bayonet.

Above: This group of soldiers is clad in wool gymnastiorki (field blouses) and furashki (visor caps). The braided cloth piping outlining some of their pogoni (shoulder boards) was characteristic for volunteers.

Right: The medic seated on the right wears an issued sherst (wool) gymnastiorka (field blouse) and a papaha (astrakhan or fleece/fur winter cap). The soldier standing on the left wears an issued gymnastiorka and furashka (visor cap). Winter, 1916.

The soldiers in this studio photo wear privately tailored sherstjanaja gymnastiorki (wool field blouses). The braided cloth piping outlining their shoulder boards was usually characteristic of volunteers, reservists, and national guardsmen.

The three soldiers in this photo wear stiffened furashki and are armed with M1881 sabers. Regimental distinctions are painted on their wool pogoni (shoulder boards). 1916.

The officer seated on the left wears a privately tailored, double breast pocketed sherst gymnastiorka made of a high quality grade of green brown wool with stiffened gold stitched shoulder boards. He has a silver plated Romanov badge pinned below his right pocket flap. His matching wool visor cap has been stiffened with either starch, cardboard, or wire. The man seated on his right wears a dark green wool three-quarter-length coat with brass buttons bearing a Romanov eagle motif. His visor cap has been stiffened but has no cockade. The soldier standing in the background wears a double-breasted dark green wool overcoat with ornately gold stitched velvet shoulder boards. Underneath his overcoat he wears a white cotton gymnastiorka, which he has belted. His visor cap is made of wool with a velvet band and has been shaped using wire. The metal insignia that he wears on the velvet band of his visor cap and on the lapels of his overcoat depict a crossed shovel and pick with two lightning bolts. Pioneers wore the crossed shovel and pick motif, and telephone/telegraph troops used the lightning bolt motif.

This soldier wears a winter overcoat made of a heavy grade of brownish gray wool (shinel) and an issued wool furashka (visor cap) with leather chin strap. The roundels on his metal cockade are painted orange and black. 1915.

The mustached soldier seated in this cabinet portrait wears a privately tailored gymnastiorka (field blouse) with two pleated exterior breast pockets. His furashka (visor cap) has been stiffened, most likely with wire.

The four infantrymen in this studio photo wear papahi (astrakhan or fleece/fur winter caps). Two of these infantrymen are armed with M1891 Mosin-Nagant rifles, the ammunition for which they carry in their cloth bandoliers and leather ammo pouches.

Above: This soldier is from the No. 298 Mstislawski Infantry Regiment, as indicated by the numbers on his shoulder boards. On his wool shoulder boards is a metal number "9" in the regimental number "298," whereby the numbers "2" and "8" have been painted on. He wears his wool, double breast-pocketed gymnastiorka (field blouse) belted. His furashka (visor cap) has a leather chinstrap and has been stiffened, most likely with wire. St. Petersburg, 1915.

Right: This soldier wears an issued sherst (wool) gymnastiorka (field blouse) that he has belted, and an issued furashka as well. He has a Romanov medal pinned to his gymnastiorka, and his unit numbers and distinctions stenciled on his wool shoulder boards. 1916.

The officer in this cabinet portrait wears a privately tailored, double breast-pocketed sherst gymnastiorka with gold stitched pogoni (shoulder boards). He has stiffened his furashka (visor cap) with either cardboard or wire. He is armed with an M1881 saber and a holstered Nagant revolver. 1916.

This soldier wears a privately tailored sherst (wool) gymnastiorka (field blouse) with two breast pockets. He has two enameled Romanov badges pinned on each button flap. He has shaped his furashka with leather chinstrap using wire. His gold stitched shoulder boards indicate his rank is roughly that of a lieutenant, or podporutschik.

The soldier seated in this cabinet portrait wears an issued sherst furashka with leather chinstrap. His visor has been painted, and his cockade has been subdued as well. He wears an issued wool gymnastiorka (field blouse) that he has belted. His woolen pogoni have been stiffened and have stenciled unit distinctions. 1916.

This group of soldiers wears a wide variety of gymnastiorki (field blouses) and furashki (visor caps), 1915.

The soldiers in this group photo wear a wide variety of gymnastiorki and furashki. Several of the soldiers have a gilded double-headed eagle badge fastened to their gymnastiorki. 1916.

These three soldiers wearing sherstjanaja (wool) furashki (visor caps) and gymnastiorki (field blouses) pose for a photo with their canine comrade. 1916

This frontovik (frontline soldier) wears an issued furashka (visor cap) and gymnastiorka (field blouse). His sharovari (dark green wool trousers) and sapogi (boots) appear issue as well. He is armed with an M1891 Mosin Nagant rifle and bayonet.

Officers visiting with their families before leaving for the front, 1914.

An officer and an NCO visiting with their families before leaving for the front. The officer standing behind the white picket fence wears a wool tunic and stiffened visor cap. The NCO leaning against the stair rail wears a privately tailored gymnastiorka that he has belted. 1914.

Chapter Four

Motor Corps

This spectacular front photo taken in 1916 captures and reflects a Russo-American symbiosis. The officer seated in the sidecar wears a privately tailored tweed tunic. He wears a round cockade and pioneer insignia on a visor cap with leather chinstrap. The rider wears a double breast-pocketed, privately tailored sherst gymnastiorka. He also has a round cockade with pioneer insignia on his furashka. The soldier of unknown rank standing in the background wears a wool tunic and visor cap with chinstrap.

The soldier in this 1916 vintage studio photo wears a privately tailored, double breast-pocketed wool gymnastiorka (field blouse) with stiff wool pogoni (shoulder boards) bearing metal motor corps and artillery insignia. He is armed with a saber.

Left: This motor corps driver wears a privately tailored leather tunic and a stiffened dark colored wool visor cap with white piping and leather chinstrap. Below the round cockade on his visor cap is a gilded Romanov double-headed eagle. Right: The motor corps driver in this 1916 studio photo wears a double breast pocketed, privately tailored sherst (wool) gymnastiorka (field blouse) belted with a single pronged buckle leather belt. Attached to his woolen shoulder boards, which are held in place by brass buttons bearing a Romanov eagle, are metal motor corps insignia. His furashka (visor cap) is made entirely of wool, with the exception of his metal oval shaped cockade, which has been covered with wool. His goggles are leather, with circular glass lenses held in place with metal frames.

This NCO wears a belted, privately tailored sherst (wool) gymnastiorka (field blouse) with two pleated exterior breast pockets. The gilded badge pinned to his left breast pocket flap and the metal insignia on his shoulder boards indicate he is an armored car driver. His gilded breast badge depicts a winged wheel, above which rests a machinegun on a tripod. This motif is framed by a wreath of leaves. His die-stamped metal shoulder board insignia is the same as the breast badge (a machinegun on a tripod resting atop a winged wheel), though only slightly smaller in size and not framed by a wreath of leaves. The mud on the chair and on his hob-nailed, lace-up leather ankle boots displays some of the harsh terrain and weather conditions on the front. The Russians used armored cars effectively throughout the First World War. The effective use of armored cars resulted in their usage to grow from Automobile Machinegun Battery (Awtomobílnaja Pulemjótnaja Bateréja) to company (róta), and finally to division (diwízia) strength by 1916.

A group of motor corps drivers pause for a photo before heading to the front in 1915. Many automobiles, such as these, were later armed with machineguns, armored with heavy iron plating at Putilov factories, and converted into Armored Cars or Automobile Machineguns (Awtomobílnaja Pulemjótnaja).

This group of motorists appears ready to take on the harsh weather conditions at the front. The two men in the back seat of the automobile wear winter overcoats made of heavy brownish gray wool (shinel). The driver and his goggled passenger wear heavy fur coats, most likely bear fur. All are relying on their furashki (visor caps) to keep their heads warm. Early winter, 1915.

Left: This motor corps driver wears a double-breasted leather tunic with matching leather trousers and wool shoulder boards (pogoni) bearing metal motor corps insignia. Right: This motor corps driver wears a privately tailored leather tunic/jacket. Motorists preferred leather gear whenever it was available, because it offered more protection against harsh weather conditions, to which they were often exposed. The roundels on his oval cockade, which he fastened to his papaha (astrakhan or fleece/fur winter cap), are painted orange and black. He is armed with a Nagant revolver and an M1881 saber. 1915.

The soldier in this 1915 vintage studio photo wears a privately tailored sherst (wool) gymnastiorka (field blouse) with dark green wool trousers, or sharovari. His woolen shoulder boards are outlined with a braided cloth border and have die-stamped metal motor corps insignia stitched to them. Motor corps insignia depicted a pair of winged wheels with a steering wheel between them.

The motorist standing in the center of this studio photo wears greenish brown wool furashka (visor cap) and a privately tailored striped wool jacket, which indicates he may be a volunteer, or there was nothing left at the depot to outfit him. The two motorists on the right and left wear leather tunics/jackets, which were preferred because of the extra protection leather offered in harsh weather conditions.

The three motor corps drivers in this studio photo wear privately tailored wool gymnastiorki. Their woolen pogoni (shoulder boards) bear metal motor corps insignia. Motor corps insignia depict a pair of winged wheels with a steering wheel between them.

Czarist civil servants and firemen in a staff car on the front. The two men in the back seat wear firemen's helmets, which were normally made of brass.

This group of motorists pauses for a photo after crossing a hastily constructed bridge on the southwest front. Following behind them is a horse drawn cart.

The Russian Red Cross, 1914.

A captured armored car. Front sjéwerny (Northern front), 1915.

Chapter Five

Artillery and Arillerists

A pre- to early-war photo of an artillerist. His headdress and his brass belt buckle bear a Romanov double-headed eagle with crossed cannon barrels motif. He proudly displays his M1881 saber. The spurs on his sapogi (boot) indicate he is most likely from the mounted or horse artillery.

Above: A group of artillerists pose for a photo with their ordinance alongside a railroad track, 1916.

Lcft: A mustached artillerist sitting on a tree stump in a snowy wood on the northern front. He has his right hand tucked inside his fleece-lined overcoat, while his left wrist rests on his M1881 saber. He has his overcoat belted with a leather belt and a brass buckle bearing a Romanov double-headed eagle with crossed cannon barrels motif. His wool shoulder boards indicate he is an NCO. His black papaha (astrakhan or fleece/fur winter cap) is the type preferred by Cossacks. The soldier in the background wears a fleece lined three-quarter-length coat and a papaha. 1915.

This artillerist wears a privately tailored sherst (wool) gymnastiorka (field blouse) with two breast pockets and dark green wool trousers, or sharovari. Among the Romanov medals pinned above his left breast pocket are a Czar Nicholas II silver bravery medal and a three hundred years of the Romanov Dynasty commemorative medal. His brass belt buckle bears a Romanov double-headed eagle with crossed cannon barrels motif. His woolen shoulder boards have die stamped crossed cannon barrel sewn to them and numbers, as well as other distinctions stenciled on them. His should boards also indicate he is an NCO. He carries an M1881, saber and the spurs on his sapogi indicate he may be from the mounted or horse artillery. 1916.

This artillery crew pauses for a photo before loading their field cannon. Front jugozápadny (Southwestern front), 1916.

Damaged and abandoned field cannons. Front sjéwerny (Northern front), 1915.

The artillerist in this 1916 vintage studio photo wears a belyo (linen) gymnastiorka and dark green sharovari. Stenciled on his woolen shoulder boards are two crossed cannon barrels and his unit numbers and distinctions. His brass belt buckle bears a Romanov double-headed eagle motif.

A pair of Imperial German manufactured 76mm Minenwerfer (trench mortars), which were possibly captured.

A group of soldiers wearing papahi (astrakhan or fleece/fur winter caps) and furashki (visor caps) gather round and stare in awe at a heavy artillery projectile. Front jugozápadny (Southwest front), 1916.

Russian soldiers clad in papahi (astrakhan or fleece/fur winter cap) and heavy winter wool overcoats (shineli) standing next to an overturned piece of 15cm Festungs Artillerie (15cm Fortress Artillery) in a snowy wood. 1916.

Soldiers of the k.u.k. Armee (imperial and royal or Austro-Hungarian Army) pose for a photo with their captured Czarist artillerists and artillery pieces.

A group of artillerists wearing various styles of furashki and gymnastiorki posing for a photo in front of a piece of heavy artillery. Southwest front, 1916.

Artillerists holding the ramrod for their heavy artillery piece pause for a photo. This photo is standard postcard size and has a green and white colored Latvian (Baltic State/Country) postage stamp on the back.

A group of artillerists pose for a photo in front of a log cabin. The artillerist standing on the right wearing the wooly black papaha cocked back on his head carries a kinjal (a knife with both sides of the blade edged).

This photo displays not only a detailed view of a heavy artillery projectile, but also a variety of winter overcoats worn by various ranks on the front, 1915.

This is a patriotic commercial photo postcard from 1914 depicting mounted artillerists transporting their field cannon and caisson to the front.

This is a patriotic commercial photo postcard from 1914 depicting artillerists loading a 76.2mm Putilov M1902 field cannon.

A group of artillerists wearing wool overcoats (shineli) and furashki (visor caps) cleaning the barrel of their 76.2mm Putilov M1902 field cannon. They have also attempted to camouflage the caissons and another 76.2mm Putilov M1902 field cannon. The back of this photo is dated October 1915.

A 76.2mm Putilov M1902 field cannon and camouflaged caisson, 1915.

A group of artillerists resting on the carriage of their 76.2mm Putilov M1902 field cannon at the edge of a snowy wood on the Northern front.

An artillerist wearing a furashka and a heavy wool overcoat (shinel) overlooks a camouflaged artillery piece atop a snow-covered ridge, 1916.

This is a patriotic commercial photo postcard from 1914 depicting artillerists wearing pre- to early-war gymnastiorki and furashki and a 76.2mm Putilov M1902 field cannon.

This is a patriotic commercial photo postcard from 1914 depicting artillerists firing their field cannon.

A group of artillerists preparing to fire their field cannon on a snow covered battlefield. They wear heavy wool winter overcoats (shineli) and black papahi (astrakhan or fleece/fur winter caps). This style of papaha was preferred by Cossacks and Siberian Regiments.

A group of artillerists wearing papahi pause for a photo that offers a breach view of their field cannon.

This is a patriotic commercial photo postcard from 1914 depicting a crew preparing to fire a mortar.

This is a patriotic commercial photo postcard from 1914 depicting artillerists standing next to their field cannon. Also visible in the background is a caisson.

A group of artillerists standing next to their field cannons.

Three artillerists wearing khlopok (cotton) gymnastiorki (field blouses) pose for a photo behind what is left of their field cannon, 1916.

This is a patriotic commercial photo postcard from 1914 depicting artillerists loading their field cannon.

A group of artillerists wearing winter overcoats (shineli) and furashki (visor caps) pose for a photo in front of their field cannon in a clearing in a snowy wood, 1915.

This is a patriotic commercial photo postcard from 1914 depicting an artillery observation post.

Four artillerists pose next to their field cannon. This photo displays an excellent side view of their field cannon. Winter 1915.

This is a patriotic commercial photo postcard from 1914 depicting artillerists and their 76.2mm Putilov M1902 field cannons.

This is a patriotic commercial photo postcard from 1914 depicting artillerists and their 76.2mm Putilov M1902 field cannons.

A group of soldiers wearing furashki (visor caps) and gymnastiorki (field blouses) preparing their artillery piece. The NCO standing on the far right, with his hands behind his back, has a Latvian Rifleman Badge pinned to the left button flap of his gymnastiorka and a metal number "5" on his woolen shoulder boards. The officer standing with one knee bent and his hands in his pockets also has a Latvian Rifleman Badge pinned to the left button flap of his gymnastiorka. He has his gymnastiorka belted with a style of belt that was normally reserved for parades or gala events, however, he has chosen to wear it in the field instead. He wears a white enameled St. George Cross for officers. This decoration is from the Order of St. George (Orden Svjatoi Georgia) and was awarded for those who displayed acts of bravery. The officer standing on the far left with his hands in his pockets also wears a white enameled St. George Cross for officers.

This is a patriotic commercial photo postcard from 1914 depicting masked artillerists preparing their field cannon.

This is a patriotic commercial photo postcard from 1914 depicting a crew preparing to fire their 76.2mm Putilov M1902 field cannon from atop a ridge. The soldiers lying side by side along the ridge display the various types of equipment carried.

These two artillerists wearing stiffened furashki and gymnastiorki pose next to armor shielded field cannon. 1916.

A group of artillerists on the front posed for a photo with their field cannon. All wear furashka (visor caps), some of which have camouflaged cockades, and gymnastiorki (field blouses) made from various materials. The mustached officer holding his binoculars wears a hooded lightweight trench coat. The artillerists in the first row hold rounds for the field cannon.

A French manufactured railwcy cannon that was abandoned by retreating Russian Forces.

This is a patriotic commercial photo postcard from 1914 depicting a line of field cannons.

Chapter Six

Guards

A pre- to early-war studio photo of a Life Guardsman. The Cyrillic script in the background reads "In Memory of My Military Service." It is also interesting to note that he wears his brass belt buckle with a Romanov double-headed eagle motif upside down.

This is a pre- to early-war cabinet portrait of a Life Guardsman. He wears a high-collared, double-breasted dark green wool tunic and stiffened shoulder boards bearing metcl Life Guard insignia. Above the oval cockade on his visor is a Romanov double-headed eagle badge. His ribbon shaped brass plaque above the Romanov eagle appears similar to those awarded to Russo-Japanese War veterans.

This Guardsman wears a privately tailored sherst (wool) gymnastiorka (field blouse) with matching wool pants. The white stripe running the length of his button flap and his white painted leather belt are a style preferred by Guardsmen. This studio photo was taken in Moscow in 1916.

A pre- to early-war cabinet portrait of three Life Guardsmen. The two Life Guardsmen standing carry a M1881 saber and wear typical Life Guard Headdress. This type of headdress was largely, but not entirely, reserved for parade or gala events.

This is a pre- to early-war photo of a Life Guardsman. He wears a double-breasted wool tunic with matching wool trousers. His leather belt has been painted white, and his brass belt buckle bears a Romanov double-headed eagle motif.

Left: This soldier wears stiffened woolen shoulder boards bearing metal Life Guard Regiment insignia. He wears a privately tailored leather tunic, which would offer more protection from harsh weather conditions than would a tunic made of cloth. His papaha appears rigid and has an oval shaped metal cockade with orange and black roundels.

This group of Guardsmen from various regiments looks as if they have come directly from the front and to the first studio for a cabinet portrait. They are clad in a variety of privately tailored gymnastiorka made from various materials; however, each Guardsmen has a cloth strip in their regimental colors running the length of their button flap. Two of the Guardsmen wear leather belts painted white. The Guardsman seated on the far right wears a regimental breast badge from the Preobrazhenski Life Guard Regiment. This breast badge was gilded and had a blue enamel "X" shaped cross with a crucified figure of St. Andrew in gold.

A pre- to early-war studio photo of a Life Guardsman. The Cyrillic script in the background reads "In Memory of My Military Service." He has a Militia Cross pinned to his double-breasted wool tunic and he carries an M1881 saber.

This is a pre- to early-war studio photo of a Life Guardsman. He wears a double-breasted wool tunic with a very distinctive cut and has belted it with a woven silk belt. This type of belt was also worn in the field to belt a gymnastiorka. Normally, headdress such as this was reserved for wearing in parades or at gala events. However, one could wear this in the field for a decadent appearance.

A pre- to early-war studio photo of two Life Guardsmen. The Guardsman on the right wears a double-breasted wool tunic. His leather belt has been painted white, and his brass belt buckle bears a Romanov double-headed eagle motif. His wool cap has a glossy visor and an oval cockade with orange and black roundels. The Guardsman also wears a double-breasted wool tunic, which he has belted with a plain brass buckled leather belt. His headdress was largely, but not entirely, reserved for wearing in parades or at gala events.

The Guardsman in this 1915 vintage studio portrait wears a stiff pillbox shaped forage cap and a privately tailored gymnastiorka (field blouse) with pogoni (shoulder boards) bearing Guard unit markings.

A pre- to early-war studio photo of a Life Guardsman. He wears a double-breasted wool tunic with a very distinctive cut. He carries an M1881 saber. His headdress was largely, but not entirely, reserved for wear in parades or at gala events.

This mustached Guardsman wears a double breast-pocketed, privately tailored sherst (wool) gymnastiorka (field blouse). His stiff sherstjanaja (wool) pogoni (shoulder boards) have a gilded Cyrillic letter and the Roman numerals "III" (Alexander III).

Chapter Seven

Cadets

A pre- to early-war studio photo of a navy cadet.

A studio photo taken in Tallinn, Estonia (Baltic State/Country), of three navy cadets.

A pre- to early-war class photo of young cadets from a military school.

A pre- to early-war class photo of young cadets from a school for military musicians.

This is a pre- to early-war cabinet portrait of three cadets. These three cadets wear double-breasted coats with brass buttons and caps with shiny visors.

A group of cadets armed with M1891 Mosin-Nagant rifles on a shooting range in southern Russia. Other firearms can be seen as well, such as an American manufactured Winchester rifle.

Seated in the center of this pre- to early-war military school class photo is a regimental priest (Batyushka) wearing two medals and three crosses. Also seated in the same row as the priest is a highly decorated officer holding an M1881 saber.

Above: A pre- to early-war studio photo of navy cadets. Tallinn, Estonia (Baltic State/Country). Below: A studio photo of cadets, Moscow, 1916.

Chapter Eight

Militia Crosses
Reservists/National Guardsmen/Volunteers

The bearded soldier seated in this cabinet portrait wears a double-breasted wool coat with rank stripes on his left sleeve. He has a marksman badge and a Romanov medal pinned to his chest, and a Militia Cross fastened to his furashka (visor cap). Soldiers serving in Siberian Regiments preferred having heavy beards, such as this man. The mustached officer seated on the left wears a wool tunic that he has belted with a woven silk belt, and a cap with black curling ringlets of wool. The young recruits have Militia Crosses fastened to their visor caps and are armed with M1891 Mosin-Nagant bolt action rifles with fixed bayonets

The soldiers in this pre- to early-war studio photo wear double-breasted tunics made of dark green wool. All three have an oval cockade with orange and black roundels and a Militia Cross fastened to their pillbox-shaped caps.

Left: This bearded soldier wears a double-breasted wool tunic with matching wool shoulder boards that have what appear to be Guard markings stenciled on them. The brass buttons on his tunic bear a flaming canon ball, indicating he is most likely a Grenadier. He has a Militia Cross fastened to his stiff wool cap, which has a shiny visor. Right: This mustached soldier wears a double-breasted dark green wool tunic with brass buttons. The buttons, as well as his brass belt buckle, bear a Romanov double-headed eagle motif. He has a Militia Cross fastened to his dark green wool furashka.

This soldier wears a double-breasted dark green wool tunic with matching dark green wool trousers, or sharovari. He carries an M1881 saber. He has an oval-shaped cockade with orange and black roundels and a Militia Cross fastened to his pilotka, a pillbox-shaped forage cap.

The soldier in this photo wears a double-breasted wool tunic with brass buttons. He has a Militia Cross attached to his stiffened visor cap and is armed with a Berdan rifle and bayonet.

The soldier in this studio photo wears a double breasted wool tunic with brass buttons and a pillbox-shaped forage cap with a Militia cross and cockade. He is armed with a Berdan rifle and bayonet.

The soldier in this studio photo taken in Moscow wears a double-breasted wool tunic with wool shoulder boards. His unit numbers and distinctions have been stenciled on his shoulder boards, which are a different grade and color of wool than the tunic. He has an oval cockade with orange and black roundels and a Militia Cross fastened to his visor cap.

Left: This officer wears a double-breasted brownish gray wool winter overcoat (shinel) with gold stitched shoulder boards bearing crossed cannon insignia. He has a rosette cockade with golden orange and black roundels and a Militia Cross fastened to his stiffened visor cap.

Below: The recruits, volunteers, national guardsmen, and reservists in this group photo carry M1891 Mosin-Nagant rifles with bayonets fixed. Most have Militia Crosses fastened to their furashki (visor caps) or their civilian headdress. This photo captures the rugged determination of the Czar Russian Armed forces.

The two soldiers in this studio photo wear double-breasted dark green wool tunics and matching dark green wool sharovari. Both wear pillbox-shaped forage caps with oval cockades, however, the soldier standing on the left wears a Militia Cross above his cockade.

The soldier holding a rifle in this studio photo wears a double-breasted wool tunic. He has an oval cockade with black and orange roundels and a Militia Cross fastened to his pillbox-shaped forage cap. The Cyrillic inscription on the plaque reads "In Memory of My Military Service."

The soldier leaning on the pedestal wears a double-breasted wool tunic with piped edges. He has an oval cockade with orange and black roundels and a Militia Cross fastened to his stiffened pillbox-shaped forage cap.

The two bearded soldiers in this studio photo wear double-breasted wool tunics with matching wool trousers. They also wear pillbox-shaped forage caps, to which they have fastened oval cockades with orange and black roundels and Militia Crosses.

This mustached soldier wears a double-breasted dark green wool tunic and a stiffened visor cap, to which he has fastened an oval cockade with orange and black roundels and a Militia Cross. The brass belt buckle on his leather belt bears a flaming canon ball motif, indicating he is a Grenadier.

The solider in this studio photo wears a double-breasted wool tunic with brass buttons. He has an oval cockade with orange and black roundels attached to his stiffened visor cap, as well as a Militia Cross.

The two NCOs in this pre- to early-war cabinet portrait wear double-breasted wool tunics with matching wool trousers. Above the cockade on their visor caps, each have fastened a Militia Cross. The NCO standing on the left has two Romanov medals pinned to his chest.

The two men in this studio photo wear double-breasted wool tunics that they have belted. They have militia Crosses fastened to their stiffened visors.

The soldier in this studio photo wears a double-breasted wool tunic with matching wool pants. He has a Militia Cross and an oval cockade with painted orange and black roundels fastened to his visor cap. Also, he has a military school badge fastened to his tunic.

Chapter Nine

The *Papaha* (*Astrakhan*, or Winter Fleece/Fur Cap)

The three soldiers in this 1915 vintage studio photo are ready for cold weather on the front! All three wear papahi with oval cockades. The NCO in the center wears a brownish gray overcoat made from a heavy grade of wool. The other two soldiers wear white fleece lined coats ideal for winter camouflage. All are armed with M1891 Mosin-Nagant rifles and wear six-pouch leather bandoliers, with each pouch carrying clips, which hold five rounds. Cloth bandoliers were also used.

Left: This soldier, with his papaha (astrakhan or fleece/fur winter caps) cocked back on his head, wears a privately tailored sherst gymnastiorka with woolen shoulder boards bearing crossed rifle insignia. He proudly displays his wood handled long curved knife, or bebout. The bebout was preferred by forward scouts and artillerists. Right: The soldier in this cabinet portrait with his papaha cocked to one side wears a roughly cut winter overcoat made of coarse wool (shinel). He has secured his wool hood/cowl, or bashlik, by tucking it under his shoulder boards and waist belt.

These three soldiers wear papahi with side flaps that unhooked and folded down for extra protection in harsh weather. Surprisingly, no one has a cockade fastened to his papaha. Their winter overcoats appear to be made from a coarse wool. The soldier standing on the left is armed with an Austro-Hungarian manufactured M1895 bayonet, and the soldier on the right is armed with bebout. The bebout was preferred by forward scouts and artillerists.

This mustached soldier wears a papaha that has a conical shape. His winter overcoat is made from a coarse wool and has had some repair done to it. He has his bashlik (hood or cowl) secured by tucking it under his shoulder boards and waist belt. He has also painted his brass belt buckle, which bears a Romanov double-headed eagle motif. 1916.

The officer in this studio photo wears a privately tailored wool tunic with a stiff collar and brass buttons bearing a Romanov double-headed eagle motif. He clutches his saber with his left hand, and in his right hand he holds his papaha. The way he holds his papaha in this photo offers a look at the inside of the cap's quilted lining.

This soldier wears a papaha with sides that unhook and fold down to protect against harsh weather conditions. He has two Romanov medals and a marksman badge pinned to his coarse wool overcoat.

The two soldiers seated in this 1915 vintage studio photo wear coarse wool winter overcoats with matching wool shoulder boards bearing their unit markings. Both have Latvian Rifleman Badges with ribbons and wear a style of papaha with sides that unhook and fold down to protect against harsh weather conditions.

Above: This group photo displays a variety of sizes and shapes of papaha, as well as a variety of tunics and gymnastiorka (field blouse). The NCO seated in the center of the second row carries an M1881 saber.

The three soldiers in this pre- to early-war cabinet portrait wear double-breasted wool tunics with matching trousers and are armed with M1881 sabers. The soldier in the center wears a pillbox shaped forage cap with a Militia Cross fastened above his cockade. The other two soldiers wear papahi (astrakhan or fleece/fur winter caps) with gilded Romanov double-headed eagle badges fastened to them.

These two soldiers in this studio photo wear an extra wooly black papaha. This style of papaha was preferred by Cossacks and soldiers serving in Siberian regiments. Both wear a roughly cut winter overcoat made of coarse wool. Their brass belt buckles bear a Romanov double-headed eagle motif.

The NCO in this studio photo wears a wooly black papaha that was preferred by soldiers serving in Siberian regiments and Cossacks. The lanyard around his neck is attached to a 7.62mm caliber seven round M1895 Nagant revolver.

This soldier wears a papaha and a coarse wool winter overcoat, and is holding a lever action 7.62mm caliber Winchester M1895 with bayonet fixed. This model was manufactured in the United States for Imperial Russia from 1914-17.

Left: The two soldiers in this 1915 vintage studio photo proudly display their M1895 bayonets for the 7.62mm caliber Winchester rifle. Both of the soldiers' papahi appear to be issued. Right: The soldier in this studio wears a white papaha and a roughly cut winter overcoat made of coarse wool. The lanyard around his neck is attached to a holstered 7.62mm caliber Nagant M1895 seven shot revolver. He carries an M1881 saber.

This soldier wears a wooly light gray papaha and a privately tailored gymnastiorka with woolen shoulder boards bearing crossed rifle insignia. He has chosen to roll up his winter overcoat or blanket and has it flung over his shoulder. Normally, he would also tuck the ends into his copper mess tin, or krushka. This was a common practice of soldiers in the Czarist Armed Forces.

Both NCOs featured on this postcard wear a style of winter cap known as an ushanka. An ushanka was similar to a papaha, but had long ear flaps that folded down for protection in harsh weather. 1915.

This group photo displays a variety of shapes, sizes, and colors of papahi. Riga, Latvia (Baltic State/Country), 1915.

The NCO seated in the center of this group wears a tall conical shaped papaha that appears to have been stiffened either with starch or cardboard. The other soldiers wear issued papaha, as well as issued gymnastiorka. Almost everyone in this photo has painted his brass belt buckle.

The two soldiers in this studio photo wear winter overcoats made from a heavy grade of wool (shinel). Both have the same collar patches, but each has a slightly different style of papaha. It is also interesting to note that their oval cockades with orange and black roundels are each positioned differently on their papaha.

The NCO seated on the right in this photo wears a wool visor cap and winter overcoat. The soldier seated on the left wears a privately tailored gymnastiorka and issued papaha, as does the soldier standing behind the NCO. The other soldier wears a leather tunic/jacket with wool shoulder boards.

The cockades of these soldiers are buried in their furry papaha. All three wear a pre- to early-war double-breasted dark green wool tunic.

The NCO leaning on the pedestal in this 1915 vintage studio photo wears a double breast-pocketed, privately tailored wool gymnastiorka and a wooly papaha cocked back on his head. He is armed with a holstered 7.62mm caliber M1895 Nagant seven-round revolver and an M1881 saber with sword knot.

The woman in this cabinet portrait wears a white fleece papaha and a dark wool tcherkessa (long wool coat). Slightly visible behind her left hand is the handle of her kinjal (Cossack crafted double-edged knife).

This NCO wears a tall papaha and a rosette cockade with golden orange and black roundels. He has gold stitched rank stripes on his wool shoulder boards. The brass buttons on his winter overcoat bear a Romanov double-headed eagle motif.

This officer wears a privately tailored wool tunic (kitel) with a silver plated military school badge pinned to the button flap of his left breast pocket. He has folded his papaha atop the pedestal in this studio photo, offering a unique view of the cap's construction. Moscow, 1916.

Left: The NCO in this cabinet portrait taken in Warszawa wears a cap with black curling ringlets of wool, to which he has fastened a Romanov double-headed eagle and an oval cockade with orange and black roundels. He carries an M1881 saber. Right: This black wooly papaha worn by the bearded officer in this studio was preferred by Cossacks and soldiers serving in Siberian regiments. The officer wears a privately tailored gray wool overcoat with brass buttons bearing a Romanov double-headed eagle motif and carries a saber with sword knot.

Above: The mustached Cossack in this studio photo wears a papaha and a dark wool tcherkessa (long wool coat) with pogoni (shoulder boards). He clutches his kinjal (Cossack crafted double-edged knife) with his left hand. Right: The Cossack in this studio photo wears a light colored papaha and tcherkessa (long wool coat). He is armed with a kinjal (Cossack crafted double-edged knife).

The Caucasian irregular in this cabinet portrait wears a black papaha and clutches a riding crop. He carries a kinjal and wears intricately crafted silver gaziri (cartridges) in the wool pouches on his tcherkessa (long wool coat).

A Cossack on the Front jugozápadny (Southwestern front). He wears a black papaha and a black wool tcherkessa.

The Cossack in this pre- to early-war vintage cabinet portrait wears intricately crafted niello silver gaziri in the wool pouches on his tcherkessa. He wears a black papaha and is armed with a finely detailed kinjal (Cossack-crafted, double-edged knife) and shaska (Cossack saber).

The papaha worn by this officer is made from the same fleece as his collar and cuff accents on his privately tailored gray wool overcoat. He is armed with a revolver, which he has holstered, and an M1881 saber.

The two soldiers in this pre- to early-war studio photo taken in Moscow wear papaha and double-breasted dark green wool tunics with matching dark green wool trousers (sharovari). The soldier on the right has a lanyard around his neck that attaches to a 7.62mm caliber Nagant M1895 seven-shot revolver. The soldier on the left is armed with a saber.

These two soldiers in this pre- to early-war studio photo wear papaha and double-breasted dark green wool tunics with matching dark green sharovari. Both wear their gray wool with overcoats over their shoulders.

The Caucasian irregular in this cabinet portrait wears a wooly black papaha and a light colored wool tcherkessa. He is armed with a kinjal and a foreign manufactured bolt action carbine with a modified sling. The back of this photo is dated February 8, 1915.

Chapter Ten

Pioneers

This pioneer holding the seat of his bicycle wears a double-breast pocketed, privately tailored sherst (wool) gymnastiorka (field blouse) and an issued furashka (visor cap) with an oval cockade, which has roundels painted orange and black. His brass belt buckle bears a Romanov double-headed eagle clutching two long handled axes in its talons. This motif is found on the belt buckles of soldiers serving in pioneer units.

The officers and NCOs in this studio photo are all armed with M1881 sabers. The metal crossed anchor and axe insignia worn on the furashki (visor caps) and shoulder boards of these soldiers indicate they are railroad pioneers.

Pre- to early-war photos of pioneers erecting a pontoon bridge across a river.

The stenciling on the woolen shoulder boards of this soldier's double breast-pocketed khlopok (cotton) gymnastiorka (field blouse) indicate he is a pioneer. He has been awarded the St. George Cross for valor and has it pinned above his right breast pocket.

Below: A pre- to early-war photo of switchboard operators and technicians.

Left: The soldier in this cabinet portrait wears a double breast-pocketed privately tailored sherst (wool) gymnastiorka (field blouse), to which he has pinned two Romanov medals. The crossed anchor and axe on his visor cap indicate he is a railroad pioneer. Right: The officer seated in this studio photo holds a M1881 saber and wears a privately tailored wool tunic with gold stitched shoulder boards. The crossed anchor and axe insignia fastened to his visor cap indicate he is a railroad pioneer.

The bearded railroad pioneer in this cabinet portrait wears a privately tailored wool tunic with gold stitched shoulder boards.

A pre- to early-war cabinet portrait of three railroad pioneers.

Left: The soldier seated in this studio photo wears a privately tailored sherst (wool) gymnastiorka (field blouse) with pleated exterior breast pockets and woolen shoulder boards bearing pioneer insignia. The soldier standing on the left wears a privately tailored gymnastiorka with cloth piping outlining his button flaps, collar, and cuffs. Right: This soldier wears a privately tailored sherst (wool) gymnastiorka (field blouse) with pleated exterior breast pockets. He has telegraph/telephone operator insignia pinned to his left button flap, 1916.

Chapter Eleven

Life on the Front and in the Trenches

These troops are from a "Shock," or "Assault" unit, and appear to be calmly awaiting an enemy advance. The soldier manning the M1905 Maxim machinegun on a Sokolov carriage with an armored shield wears an Adrian helmet, as do two of his comrades. Adrian helmets were manufactured in France, and many were exported to Imperial Russia; however, the amount exported was not sufficient. As the war progressed, Russia was able to begin manufacturing variants of the French Adrian helmet. The helmets worn here are without Romanov double-headed eagle badges, and appear to be painted in a greenish brown color, whereby earlier French manufactured models were painted blue. Southwestern Front.

Above: This outstanding action photo displays a group of soldiers fearlessly pursuing the enemy over mountainous terrain. Below: The soldiers in this group photo wear winter overcoats (shineli) and furashki (visor caps). Front and center are the bravery medal winners in this group, as well as two M1905 Maxim machineguns on Sokolov carriages with armored shields.

Above: A Danish manufactured M1904 Madsen. Below: Five officers wearing furashki (visor caps) and wool winter overcoats (shineli) prepare to greet a lady. The officer standing on the porch step (right) wears a fleece lined polushubok with a large chest pocket that buttons shut. All officers seen hear carry a M1881 saber.

A group of officers and NCOs took off their skis to pose for a photo in the ice and snow on the Northern front. The officer standing on the right wears a papaha (astrakhan or fleece/fur winter cap) with side flaps that unhook and fold down for protection against harsh weather conditions, and a fur lined polushubok, or long overcoat, with a large chest pocket that buttons shut.

This NCO holds an M1868 Russian Berdan I rifle and wears a privately tailored wool tunic with woolen shoulder boards outlined in braided cloth piping. The Berdan rifle was designed by General Hiram Berdan, and was manufactured first in England and later by Imperial Russian arms manufacturers. In addition, there was a Russian M1870 Berdan II Dragoon rifle and a M1870 Berdan II Cossack rifle. The Dragoon rifle was issued to mounted infantry, and was similar to the infantry rifle (only shorter in length). The Cossack rifle was issued to cavalry units and had a very distinctive looking trigger.

Above: A group of frontoviki (frontline troops) wearing furashki (visor caps) and Adrian-style steel helmets pause for a photo on a surrealistic battleground.
Below: A group of frontoviki (front line troops) pause for a photo, offering a glimpse of what life in the trenches was like in 1915.

Two frontoviki (frontline troops) pose for a photo outside of their dugout. Both are armed with sabers and have Latvian Rifleman badges fastened to their gymnastiorki (field blouses).

Above: Officers and NCOs visiting with Russian country folk, 1915. Below: This group of soldiers has decided to pause for a photo and a smoke. Front jugozápadny (Southwestern front), 1916.

A group of frontoviki (front line troops) in 1916. They have been issued a variety of gasmasks, including the Koumant-Zelinski Model, which is worn by the frontovik standing in the far right corner. The Koumant-Zelinski Model was made in 1916 and consisted of a rectangular shaped respirator canister and a rubber hood with lenses for the eyes that fit over the soldier's head.

This group of frontoviki (front line troops) clad in winter caps and overcoats are having their papers checked. Front sjéwerny (Northern front), 1915.

Troops arriving by train from Siberia in 1916. Below: Two officers standing outside a log cabin on the Front sjéwerny (Northern front). The officer on the right wears the Order of St. Vladimir (Orden Svjatoi Vladimira) with swords. Empress Catherine I instituted this decoration in 1783.

This group of soldiers is preparing to deploy by rail to the Front sjéwerny (Northern front), 1916.

After the battle. Front sjéwerny (Northern front), 1916.

Above: The soldiers in this group photo are armed with Japanese manufactured Arisaka rifles. Front jugozápadny (Southwestern front), 1916. Below: This group of soldiers resting at the edge of a forest on the Front sjéwerny (Northern front) is armed with Japanese manufactured Arisaka rifles. The officer lying on the ground smoking a cigarette wears a gilded and enameled Order of St. Anne (Svjatoi Anny Orden) with swords.

Above: This group of frontoviki (frontline soldiers) pauses for a photo and a bite to eat from whatever is in their krushki (copper mess kits). Many Imperial Russian manufactured shovels, such as the one shown here in this photo, were captured and used by the Imperial German armed forces. 1915.

Left: This group of frontoviki (frontline troops) is clad in papahi (astrakhan or fleece/fur winter caps) and furashki (visor caps). Front sjéwerny (Northern front), 1915.

In addition to displaying a variety of shapes and sizes of papahi (astrakhan or fleece/fur winter caps), this photo exhibits the harsh weather conditions that were endured on the front. The soldier lying on the snow-covered ground on the right holds a gas mask canister, and the soldier kneeling beside him holds a copper mess kit, or krushka.

Christmas 1915.

The soldiers in this forest wear a wide variety of visor caps and field blouses. In addition, all carry M1881 sabers.

The soldiers seen here have all been issued gasmasks in canvas bags. This photo also displays a variety of visor caps and field blouses. Front jugozápadny (Southwestern front), 1916.

Front jugozápadny (Southwestern front), 1916.

Front jugozápadny (Southwestern front), 1916.

Left: This officer is from a Hussar regiment and is wearing a fleece-lined tunic, which protected against the harsh weather conditions, such as those seen in this photo. Front sjéwerny (Northern front), 1915.

Bottom: A group of frontoviki (frontline troops) pause for a photo during a brief cease-fire. The mustached frontovik (frontline soldier) in the center wears an Adrian style steel helmet. Front jugozápadny (Southwestern front), 1916.

These frontoviki (front line troops) are enjoying some song and dance in a wooded area near the front. Many of these frontoviki wear Adrian steel helmets with Romanov double-headed eagle badges fastened to the front of their helmets. In addition, many in this group have been awarded St. George Crosses (Svjatoi Georggi Orden) for valor.

This group of soldiers is ready for a winter at the front, as most of those seen here are clad in winter overcoats (shineli). Many of the soldiers seen in this group photo have Romanov double-headed eagle badges fastened to the front of their Adrian steel helmets.

This group of frontoviki (front line troops) is preparing to fire two gas-operated Colt/Browning M1895/1914 machineguns. These guns were nicknamed "potato diggers" because during repeated firing, the heavy operating lever caused the tripod to burrow itself in the ground. The Russians referred to units armed with these machineguns as Kolta.

This photo was taken by a Latvian photographer depicting frontoviki (front line troops) in full battle dress courageously advancing over barbed wire fortifications.

Soldiers from various branches of the Czarist Russian Armed Forces are represented in this photo.

The officers and NCOs in this photo wear a wide variety of tunics and visor caps. Two of the officers have been awarded the St. George Cross (Svjatoi Georggi Orden) for valor. Front jugozápadny (Southwestern front), 1916.

Officers and NCOs clad in a variety of overcoats and visor caps pose for a group photo. Front sjéwerny (Northern front), 1915.

A group of officers and NCOs pose for a photo outside of a bunker. The officer seated on the ground next to the accordion player wears a gilded and enameled Order of St. Vladimir (Orden Svjatoi Vladimira) with swords.

A group of Latvian Riflemen with Riflemen Badges pinned to their gymnastiorki (field blouses). The Rifleman seated in the center wears a captured Imperial German pickelhaube, or spiked helmet.

Officers, NCOs, and enlisted rank soldiers pose for a group photo in a wooded area near the front, 1915.

Two mounted Cossacks and other infantry soldiers pose for a photo on a dirt road with their two captured k.u.k. (imperial and royal) Austro-Hungarian soldiers, 1915.

The regimental cooks preparing a meal in their field kitchen. Front jugozápadny (Southwestern front), 1916.

Many of the soldiers in this group photo wear Romanov double-headed eagle badges attached to their Adrian steel helmets and have been awarded the St. George Cross (Svjatoi Georggi Orden) for valor. This photo was taken in Latvia (Baltic State/Country).

Several of the soldiers seen in this group photo have been awarded the St. George Cross (Svjatoi Georggi Orden) for valor and are armed with M1881 sabers. March 23, 1916.

A group of machine gunners pauses for a meal in a grass covered field on the Front jugozápadny (Southwestern front). This photo displays a variety of krushki (copper mess tins) used by the Czarist Russian armed forces, 1916.

A group of frontoviki (frontline troops) pause for a photo on the Front sjéwerny (Northern front). The frontovik (frontline soldier) standing near the center with his hand on his bicycle has been awarded the St. George Cross (Svjatoi Georggi Orden) for valor. The frontovik kneeling on the left wears an Adrian style steel helmet.

A group of frontoviki (frontline troops) pause for a photo on the Front jugozápadny (Southwestern front). Several of these frontoviki have been awarded the St. George Cross (Svjatoi Georggi Orden) for valor.

Three officers standing in a snowy clearing on the Northern front (Front sjéwerny). All three carry the Koumant-Zelinski Model gasmask, which was made in 1916. The Koumant-Zelinski Model consisted of a rectangular-shaped respirator canister and a rubber hood with lenses for the eyes that fit over the soldier's head. The officers are dressed in appropriate attire for the harsh weather conditions seen in this photo.

A group of Latvian Rifleman pause for a photo and a drink. Most of the men have Latvian Rifleman Badges pinned to their gymnastiorki (field blouses), and others have been awarded the St. George Cross (Svjatoi Georggi Orden) for valor.

A group photo of Signal Corps and Telephone/Telegraph troops. Many of the field telephones used by these troops during the war were imported from other countries. 1915.

Russian grenades. Front jugozápadny (Southwestern front), 1916.

This group of frontoviki (frontline troops) wearing papahi (astrakhan or fleece/fur winter caps) and furashki (visor caps) pause for a photo on the front. The frontovik (frontline soldier) in the center wears a papaha (astrakhan or fleece/fur winter cap) and is preparing to speak into the receiver of a field telephone. The Czarist Russian armed forces used various models and manufactures of field telephones, many of which were imported from other countries, such as Sweden.

These two frontoviki (frontline troops) wear Adrian style helmets with Romanov double-headed eagle badges fastened to the front and brownish gray wool overcoats (shineli), 1916.

This group of soldiers pauses for a drink, and perhaps a little target practice in the countryside. The decorated soldier seated in the center with his legs crossed carefully aims his revolver. The soldier seated next to him on the right is from the k.u.k. (imperial and royal) Austro-Hungarian armed forces. He wears a Schiffchen (forage cap) and holds the rank of Feldwebel (sergeant). 1916.

This group of frontoviki (frontline troops) is clad in shineli (wool overcoats), and many wear Adrian style helmets with Romanov double-headed eagle badges fastened to the front. The two frontoviki seated in the first row on the left have the St. George Cross (Svjatoi Georggi Orden) for valor fastened to their shineli. In addition, many are armed with Japanese manufactured Arisaka rifles. Front sjéwerny (Northern front), 1916.

These advancing troops are armed with a variety of firearms, such as American manufactured Winchester rifles, Japanese manufactured Arisaka rifles, and Russian manufactured Mosin-Nagant rifles.

Chapter Twelve

P.O.W.s

A soldier of the k.u.k. (imperial and royal) Austro-Hungarian army standing watch over Russian Kriegsgefangenen (P.O.W.s) on the Front jugozápadny (Southwestern Front).

Soldiers of the k.u.k. (imperial and royal) Austro-Hungarian army standing watch over Russian Kriegsgefangenen (P.O.W.s). Three of the Kriegsgefangenen are Cossacks.

An officer of the k.u.k. (imperial and royal) Austro-Hungarian Army lighting a cigarette for a Russian Kriegsgefanger (P.O.W.).

Soldiers of the k.u.k. (imperial and royal) Austro-Hungarian army standing watch over Russian Kriegsgefangenen (P.O.W.s). Many of these P.O.W.s have been given k.u.k. (imperial and royal) Austro-Hungarian army enameled mess kits. In addition, they have removed the oval cockades with orange and black roundels from their furashki (visor caps).

Soldiers of the k.u.k. (imperial and royal) Austro-Hungarian army, as well as an Imperial German Kraftfahrer (Motor Corps/Motorist), standing watch over Russian Kriegsgefangenen (P.O.W.s).

Soldiers of the k.u.k. (imperial and royal) Austro-Hungarian army standing watch over Russian Kriegsgefangenen (P.O.W.s) in a makeshift Kriegsgefangenenlager (P.O.W. Camp) on the Front jugozápadny (Southwestern front). On the back of this photo is written "Russ. Ostern 1917" (Russian Easter 1917).

Soldiers of the k.u.k. (imperial and royal) Austro-Hungarian army leading blindfolded Russian Kriegsgefangenen (P.O.W.s) through barbed wire covered trenches on the Front jugozápadny (Southwestern front).

Surrendering Russian Forces in 1915.

Russian Kriegsgefangenen (P.O.W.s) weaving straw baskets in an Imperial German Kriegsgefangenenlager (P.O.W. Camp).

Russian Kriegsgefangenen (P.O.W.s) weaving straw footwear in a k.u.k. (imperial and royal) Austro-Hungarian Kriegsgefangenenlager (P.O.W. Camp).

Russian Kriegsgefangenen (P.O.W.s) in an Imperial German Kriegsgefangenenlager (P.O.W. Camp).

An enlisted rank soldier from the Czarist Russian Armed forces and an enlisted rank soldier in the k.u.k. (imperial and royal) Austro-Hungarian Armed forces pose together in this cabinet portrait.

Russian Kriegsgefangenen (P.O.W.s) preparing to shake hands in a k.u.k. (imperial and royal) Austro-Hungarian Kriegsgefangenenlager (P.O.W. Camp). On the back of this photo is written in German "Armenier," or Armenians. Armenians served in the Czarist Russian forces during the First World War.

Below: Russian Kriegsgefangenen in a k.u.k. (imperial and royal) Austro-Hungarian Kriegsgefangenenlager.

Transporting Russian Kriegsgefangenen, 1915.

Below: Soldiers of the k.u.k. (imperial and royal) Austro-Hungarian army standing watch over Russian Kriegsgefangenen.

Soldiers of the Czarist Russian Armed Forces and the k.u.k. (imperial and royal) Austro-Hungarian Armed Forces celebrate Christmas in the field, 1915.

Soldiers of the k.u.k. (imperial and royal) Austro-Hungarian army standing watch over Russian Kriegsgefangenen.

Chapter Thirteen

Cossacks and Caucasian Irregulars

High ranking Cossacks meeting with Imperial German Generals Hindenburg (left) and Ludendorff (right).

Above: Front jugozápadny (Southwestern Front), 1916.

Left: A Caucasian irregular with his papaha (astrakhan or fleece/fur winter cap) cocked back on his head fiercely clutching his kinjal (Caucasian-crafted, double-edged knife) in this studio photo.

A studio photo of a Cossack officer. He wears finely crafted niello silver gaziri, or cartridges, and gold stitched shoulder boards fastened to his tcherkessa (long wool coat). He is armed with a kinjal (Cossack-crafted, double-edged knife) and shashka (Cossack-crafted saber without hand-guard).

A studio photo of a Caucasian irregular and his family. He wears finely crafted niello silver gaziri (cartridges) and a tcherkessa (long wool coat). He is armed with an intricately designed kinjal and shashka.

This Cossack officer wears a very wooly papaha (astrakhan or fleece/fur winter cap), a style preferred by many Cossacks. The braided lanyard around his neck is fastened to his holstered revolver.

A studio photo of a Caucasian irregular and his wife. He carries a kinjal and wears intricately crafted silver gaziri (cartridges) in the wool pouches on his tcherkessa (long wool coat).

The Caucasian irregular leaning on the pedestal in this cabinet portrait wears finely crafted niello silver gaziri and is armed with a kinjal (Caucasian-crafted, double-edged knife).

The Cossack clutching his kinjal (Cossack-crafted, double-edged knife) in this cabinet portrait wears a white wool tcherkessa (long wool coat) with sixteen cylindrical wool chest pouches that hold his silver gaziri, or cartridges.

The woman and child in this cabinet portrait are dressed in Cossack garb and are clutching traditional Caucasian edged weapons.

This is a cabinet portrait of a Caucasian irregular and his wife. He wears intricately crafted silver gaziri in the wool pouches on his tcherkessa.

A studio portrait of a Caucasian irregular and his family. He wears an intricately crafted kinjal (double-edged knife) and silver gaziri in the wool pouches on his tcherkessa.

The Cyrillic inscription on this postcard-size photo reads "Hetman Pavlo Skoropadski." He has a St. George Cross (Svjatoi Georggi Orden) for valor pinned to his chest.

A cabinet portrait of a Caucasian NCO. He wears a dark colored tcherkessa with woolen pogoni (shoulder boards).

A cabinet portrait of a Cossack and his wife. He wears intricately crafted niello silver gaziri in the wool pouches on his tcherkessa, and is armed with a kinjal (Cossack-crafted, double-edged knife).

The Cossack in this pre- to early-war vintage cabinet portrait wears intricately crafted niello silver gaziri (cartridges) in the wool pouches on his tcherkessa (long wool coat). He is armed with a finely detailed kinjal (Cossack-crafted, double-edged knife) and shaska (Cossack saber).

A group of Cossacks clad in tcherkesski (long wool coats) pose for a studio photo. Each Cossack is armed with a kinjal.

Cossacks and Caucasian irregulars.

A studio photo of a Cossack and his wife. He wears a wooly beige papaha (astrakhan or fleece/fur winter cap) and a wool tcherkessa.

The couple in this studio photo are clad in light colored papahi and tcherkessi. Each carries a uniquely crafted riding crop and kinjal.

This is a cabinet portrait of a Caucasian irregular and his wife. He wears intricately crafted niello silver gaziri in the wool pouches on his tcherkessa.

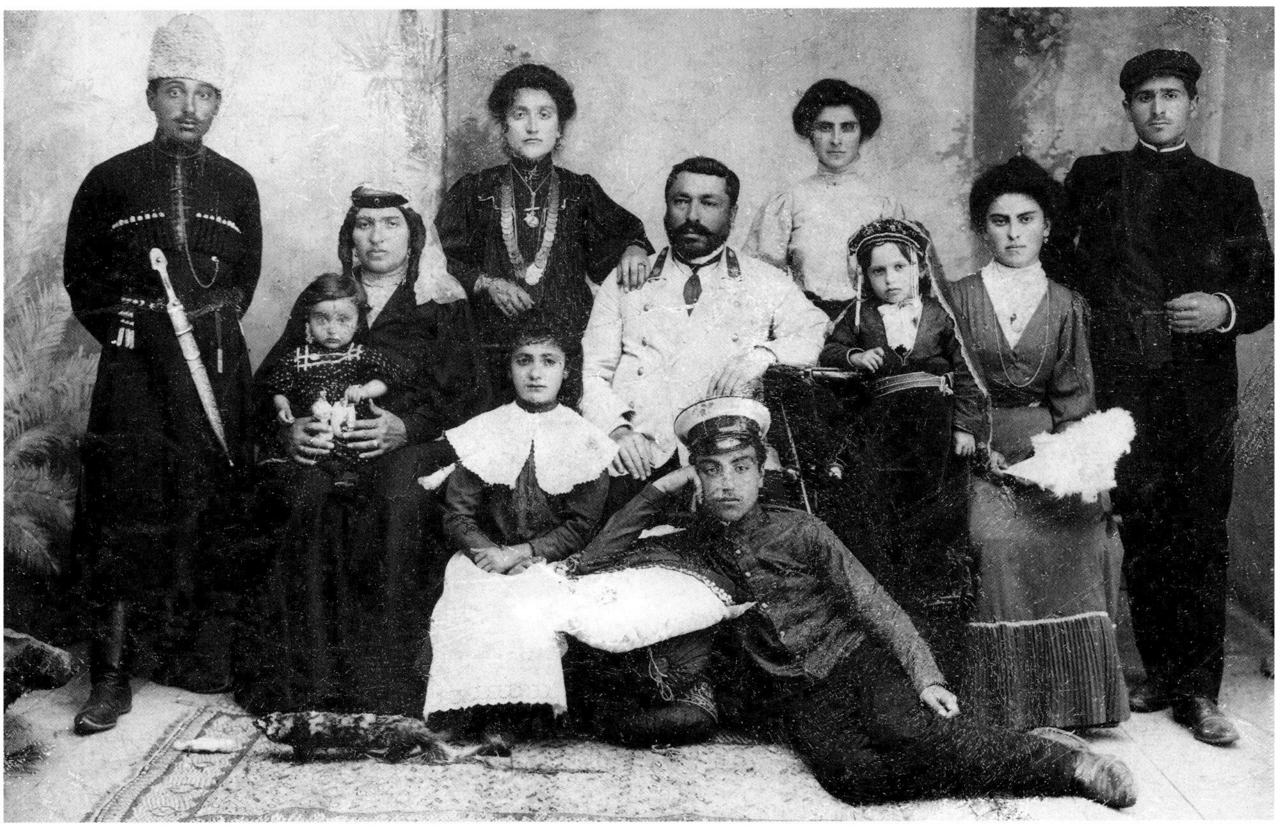

A pre- to early-war photo of a Caucasian irregular and his relatives.

A studio portrait of a Caucasian irregular and his family. He wears a kinjal and intricately crafted niello silver gaziri in the wool pouches on his tcherkessa.

A studio photo of a Cossack officer and his relatives. He wears a dark wool tcherkessa (long wool coat) to which he has fastened gold stitched pogoni (shoulder boards). He is armed with a finely crafted, ivory handled kinjal (Cossack-crafted, double-edged knife) and a shaska (Cossack saber). 1914.

These two Cossacks wear intricately crafted niello silver gaziri (cartridges) in the wool pouches on their tcherkessi (long wool coats). Each carries a unique kinjal (Cossack-crafted, double-edged knife) as well.

The six Cossacks featured in this photograph wear wool tcherkessi and black papahi. Each is armed with a uniquely crafted kinjal and shashka. The two Cossacks seated on the bench have been awarded the St. George Cross (Svjatoi Georggi Orden) for valor.

Chapter Fourteen

Cavalry, Mounted Troops, Wagons, and Sleighs

A cabinet portrait of a Hussar, Minsk 1914.

The Czarevich Alexis (Son of Czar Nicholas II) dressed as colonel of the Nizhni-Novogorod Dragoons.

A pre- to early-war studio photo of a lancer (ulánski). The brass buttons on his wool tunic bear a Romanov double- headed eagle motif, and his visor cap has been stiffened with either cardboard or wire. He proudly displays his M1881 saber.

A mounted officer armed with a saber on the Northern front (Front sjéwerny).

This mounted officer is armed with an M1881 saber. Front jugozápadny (Southwestern front), 1916.

The officer leaning on the horse drawn carriage wearing a fur trimmed tunic is from a Hussar Regiment. Northern front (Front sjéwerny).

These supplies, wagons, and horses from the Russian countryside have been conscripted for military service. Front jugozápadny (Southwestern front), April 1915.

A mounted NCO armed with a saber. Front jugozápadny (Southwestern front), 1916.

Mounted Siberian and Cossack officers, 1915.

Soldiers wearing stiffened furashki (visor caps) pause for a photo while shodding and feeding their horses. Front jugozápadny (Southwestern front), 1916.

A horse drawn field kitchen. Front jugozápadny (Southwestern front), 1916.

Officers and their canine companion riding in a horse drawn open sleigh on the Front sjéwerny (Northern front) in 1915.

Soldiers wearing gymnastiorki (field blouses) and furashki (visor caps) stand next to their supply wagons on the Front jugozápadny (Southwestern front), 1916.

This cavalryman is prepared to fight from behind the body of his horse. Front jugozápadny (Southwestern front), 1916.

The First Petrograd female mounted battalion.

Above: Before a Charge. Front sjéwerny (Northern front).

Left: A pre- to early-war studio photo of a lancer (ulánski). The brass buttons on his wool tunic bear a Romanov double-headed eagle motif, and his pillbox-shaped forage cap has been stiffened with either cardboard or wire.

Supply wagons headed for the front, 1916.

Three soldiers pause for a photo before riding off for the front. All three wear gray papaha (astrakhan or fleece/fur winter cap) and have cloth ammo bandoliers flung over their shoulders, 1915.

This mounted Cossack wears a black wool papaha (astrakhan or fleece/fur winter cap) and a wool Tcherkessa (long wool coat). He has been awarded two classes of the St. George Cross (Svjatoi Georggi Orden) for valor. His horse is muzzled with either a feed bag or gas mask.

Chapter Fifteen

Air Service

This pilot and his comrades have either crash-landed or are attempting to camouflage this pusher biplane, which is mostly of foreign manufacture. Whatever the circumstances may be, this rare photo is clearly focused and offers a detailed view of the plane's nose markings and overall construction. In addition, the proudly posed wool shrouded pilot in a bear fur-lined leather flight suit has placed his padded leather flight helmet on the lower wing and his fleece lined flight gloves in front of the windshield while his comrades try to maneuver through the trees and bushes.

Above: A group of pilots pose in front of their monoplane, which is most likely foreign manufactured, along with their ground crew. Moscow, 1915.
Below: A Farman pusher biplane, Moscow, 1914.

Moscow 1914.

A pre- to early-war photo of a group of soldiers observing a balloon flight in Moscow.

A pre- to early-war photo of a group of soldiers observing a balloon flight in Moscow.

Above: A pre- to early-war ENV airsnip factory in Moscow. Below: A pre- to early-war ENV airship factory in Moscow.

A pre- to early-war Gnome airplane engine factory in Moscow.

A pre- to early-war Gnome airplane engine factory in Moscow.

Moscow 1914.

This lucky pilot wearing a leather flight jacket and cap poses in front of the painted red, blue, and white roundel on the fuselage of his overturned biplane. Even when having the benefit of an open field, landing was very difficult and often resulted in causalities. Officers and other ranks have also chosen to be photographed with this spectacle. 1916.

This soldier wears a privately tailored sherst (wool) gymnastiorka (field blouse) with two pleated breast pockets. His stiff woolen pogoni (shoulder boards) bear a metal winged anchor insignia and metal numbers "3" and "5," indicating he is a balloonist from the 35th balloon company.

The aviator in this cabinet portrait wears a privately tailored gymnastiorka (field blouse) with pleated breast pockets. In addition, his wool pogoni (shoulder boards) bear a metal winged propeller and the number "4" insignia.

The soldier in this studio photo wears a privately tailored gymnastiorka (field blouse) with stiff pogoni (shoulder boards) bearing a metal winged propeller insignia, indicating he is an aviator. He has stiffened his furashka (visor cap) with either cardboard or wire. May 17, 1915.

Chapter Sixteen

Navy/Marines

A pre- to early-war photo of the submarine "Crocodile" and her crew off the coast of Estonia (Baltic State/Country).

A commercial photo of the first Russian submarine, the 1904 N. "Apostoli" No. 112.

The sailors posed with their families in this studio photo are from the "Oleg." Tallinn, Estonia (Baltic State/Country), 1914.

Sailors on board the Battleship Sevastopol. The Cyrillic inscription on their cap ribbons reads "Sevastopol." 1915.

This group of sailors is from the Battleship Sevastopol, as the Cyrillic writing on their cap bands indicates. 1915.

The bearded sailor in this studio photo is from the Battleship Peter the Great. The Cyrillic inscription on his cap ribbon reads "Peter the Great." 1915.

The sailor in this studio photo is from the "Oleg," as the Cyrillic writing on his cap ribbon indicates. 1914.

A sailor on board the Battleship Sevastopol. The Cyrillic inscription on his cap ribbon reads "Sevastopol." 1915.

The sailor in this studio photo is from the ship "Khabarovsk," as the Cyrillic writing on his cap ribbon indicates. Tallinn, Estonia (Baltic State/Country), 1915.

Sailors on board the Battleship Sevastopol. The Cyrillic inscription on their cap ribbons read "Sevastopol." 1915.

Tallinn, Estonia (Baltic State/ Country), 1915.

The two sailors leaning on the anchor in this cabinet portrait are from the "Iorab." 1914.

Sailors from the Battleship Sevastopol enjoying a carousel ride, 1915.

The mustached officer in this pre- to early-war vintage cabinet portrait is armed with an ivory handled kortik (dirk or dagger). In addition, he has a porcelain cockade on his wool visor cap.

Above: Sailors on skis from the Battleship Sevastopol, 1915. Below: This is a fantastic studio collage photo of a sailor from the Battleship Sevastopol, 1915.

This cabinet portrait was taken in Kronstadt in 1914. The Cyrillic inscription on the sailor's cap ribbon indicates he is from the ship the Iliad in the Baltic Fleet.

Above: Sailors from the Battleship "Sevastopol" in August 1915. Below: The two sailors in this studio photo are from the Battleship Sevastopol. Tallinn, Estonia (Baltic State/Country), 1915.

The crew of this Imperial battleship pose for a group photo inside her engine room.

A sailor from the ship Truthful, or True. Tallinn, Estonia (Baltic State/ Country), 1915.

The sailor leaning on the pedestal in this 1915 vintage studio photo is from the ship Iorab.

Chapter Seventeen

Musicians

These military bandsmen wear sherstjanaja (wool) furashki (visor caps) and gymnastiorki (field blouses), 1917.

The military bandsmen in this studio photo wear sherstjanaja (wool) furashki (visor caps) and gymnastiorki (field blouses). Several of the bandsmen have cloth musician insignia stitched on the sleeve of their gymnastiorki.

Military Marching Band, Estonia (Baltic State/Country), 1917.

Above: Members of a military marching band pose for a group photo. Several of the men in this photo have been awarded the St. George Cross (Svjatoi Georggi Orden) for valor and other Romanov medals. Below: Russian Kriegsgefanger (P.O.W.s) enjoying music and dance, 1916.

A military marching band on the front in the winter of 1916. Many of the bandsmen wear Romanov medals.

A military marching band playing for the troops on the Front jugozápadny (Southwestern Front) in 1916.

A military marching band in 1913.

A military marching band poses for a photo outside of their barracks, 1917.

Chapter Eighteen

Pre- to Early-War

A pre- to early-war cabinet portrait of an enlisted rank soldier and his wife. He wears a single-breasted dark green wool tunic and matching dark green trousers, or sharovari. He is armed with a M1891 Mosin-Nagant rifle and wears a cloth bandolier that holds the ammunition.

The three soldiers in this pre- to early-war vintage cabinet portrait wear double-breasted dark green wool tunics and matching dark green wool trousers or sharovari. The number "24" is stenciled on the dark wool band of their visor caps, which is most likely for the Simbirski Infantry Regiment.

The soldier on the bicycle in this cabinet portrait wears a double-breasted dark green wool tunic and dark green wool sharovari. The braided cloth piping outlining his woolen shoulder boards was usually indicative of volunteers.

The soldier holding his M1881 saber wears a khlopok (cotton) gymnastiorka (field blouse), which he has belted with a leather belt painted white. He has an oval-shaped cockade with orange and black roundels fastened to the red wool band of his pilotka, or pillbox-shaped forage cap.

Brandishing his M1881 saber, this soldier wears a double-breasted dark green wool tunic and matching dark green wool trousers (sharovari). He stands next to an armored shield on a two-wheel carriage.

The mustached officer in this studio photo has a military school badge pinned to his double-breasted wool tunic. His cloth armband indicates he is in a military police branch of the armed forces.

The mustached NCO in this studio photo has a rosette cockade and gilded Romanov double-headed eagle fastened to his visor cap. He wears a double-breasted dark green wool tunic and carries a saber.

The NCO in this pre- to early-war photo wears a double-breasted dark green wool tunic and carries an M1881 saber.

The NCO in this cabinet portrait wears a cylindrical cap covered with black curling ringlets of wool. He wears a double-breasted dark green wool tunic and carries an M1881 saber with sword knot. The lanyard around his neck is fastened to his holstered revolver.

Above: The soldier in this cabinet portrait wears a double-breasted dark green wool tunic and a cylindrical cap covered with black curling ringlets of wool. He has the number "38" stenciled on his woolen shoulder boards (pogoni), indicating he is from the Tobolski Infantry Regiment. Above Right: This soldier has a gilded badge fastened to his double-breasted dark green wool tunic. His wool shoulder boards (pogoni) are outlined with braided cloth piping. His cylindrical cap is covered with black curling ringlets of wool. Right: The solider in this pre- to early-war vintage cabinet portrait wears a double-breasted wool tunic and carries an M1881 saber.

The two soldiers seated in this cabinet portrait are armed with M1881 sabers. The soldier standing behind them has been awarded a marksman badge. All wear double-breasted dark green wool tunics with matching dark green wool trousers (sharovari), and have oval cockades and Romanov doubled-headed eagle badges fastened to their stiffened visor caps.

The mustached soldier in this pre- to early-war vintage cabinet portrait is from the No. 48 Odesski Infantry Regiment, and wears a double-breasted wool tunic with brass buttons bearing a Romanov double-headed eagle motif. There was also a No. 10 Odesski Lancer Regiment (ulánski polk).

The two soldiers in this studio photo have Romanov medals and marksmen badges fastened to their double-breasted dark green wool tunics.

This soldier has a brass ribbon with a Cyrillic inscription which translates "for merit" fastened above the oval shaped cockade on his pilotka (pillbox shaped forage cap). In addition, he has two Romanov medals fastened to his double-breasted dark green wool tunic.

This officer wears a double-breasted wool tunic with brass buttons bearing a Romanov double-headed eagle motif. He has been awarded the officer's white enameled St. George Cross (Svjatoi Georggi Orden) for valor.

The soldiers in this photo wear stiffened visor caps and have Romanov medals pinned to their double-breasted wool tunics.

A gendarme enjoying a drink with his friends near a stone bridge.

The soldier in this studio portrait wears a double-brecsted wool tunic with brass buttons. The leather strap across his chest holas his saber.

The soldier in this pre- to early-war vintage cabinet portrait wears a double-breasted dark green wool tunic with matching trousers (sharovari), which he has tucked into his sapogi, or boots. The metal numbers on his shoulder boards (pogoni) indicate he is from the No. 49 Brestski Infantry Regiment.

The soldier seated in this cabinet portrait is from the No. 151 Pjatigorski Infantry Regiment, as the stenciled numbers on his stiff wool shoulder boards (pogoni) indicate.

Above: The soldiers in this group photo wear winter wool overcoats (shineli) and are armed with M1881 sabers.
Below: Two officers visiting with their family.

Medics at a railway station.

The soldier posed with his family in this pre- to early-war vintage cabinet portrait is from the No. 190 Otschakowski Infantry Regiment.

The gendarme seated at the table is ready to enjoy a drink with his friends.

The soldier in this cabinet portrait wears a cylindrical cap covered with curling ringlets of black wool and proudly displays his M1881 saber. The lanyard around his neck is attached to his holstered revolver.

The three soldiers in this cabinet portrait are from the No. 195 Orowajski Infantry Regiment, as the stenciled numbers on their visor caps and shoulder boards indicate.

The soldier in this extraordinary pre- to early-war cabinet portrait wears a double-breasted dark green wool tunic and a cylindrical cap covered with dark curling ringlets of wool. Attached to his cap are a Romanov double-headed eagle badge and a brass commemorative ribbon similar to those given to Russo-Japanese war participants.

Chapter Nineteen

St. George Cross Recipients and other Decorations

The mustached officer in this cabinet portrait has two enameled, gilded, and diamond facetted Order of St. Anne (Svjatoi Anny Orden) decorations, as well as three Romanov medals fastened to his privately tailored tunic (kitel). In addition, he wears an enameled, gilded, and diamond facetted Order of St. Anne neck decoration and carries an Order of St. Anne saber. The Duke of Holstein-Gottorp, Karl Frederick, founded the order of St. Anne in 1735. He founded it to honor his wife, Anna Petrovna, who was the daughter of Peter the Great. It was the first foreign order for merit to be adopted by Russia.

This group of frontoviki (front line soldiers) wecring furashki (visor caps) and shineli (winter overcoats) have placed their comrades, who have been awarded the St. George Cross (Svjatoi Georggi Orden) for valor, in the front row. Front sjéwerny (Northern Front), 1915.

The soldier smoking the cigar standing second from the right has been awarded the St. George Cross (Svjatoi Georggi Orden) for valor. Front jugozápadny (Southwestern Front), 1916.

This group of frontoviki (front line soldiers) wearing furashki (visor caps) and gymnastiorki (field blouses) have placed their comrades, who have been awarded the St. George Cross (Svjatoi Georggi Orden) for valor, in the front row. Front jugozápadny (Southwestern Front), 1916.

The two seated Latvian Riflemen, as well as their comrade standing between them, have been awarded the St. George Cross (Svjatoi Georggi Orden) for valor. Front sjéwerny (Northern Front), 1915.

Right: The soldier in this studio portrait has been awarded the St. George Cross (Svjatoi Georggi Orden) for valor. The lanyard around his neck is attached to his 7.62mm caliber M1895 Nagant seven round revolver. He also carries a M1881 saber.

Below: Although prisoners of war, two of these men have decided to keep wearing their St. George Cross (Svjatoi Georggi Orden) for valor.

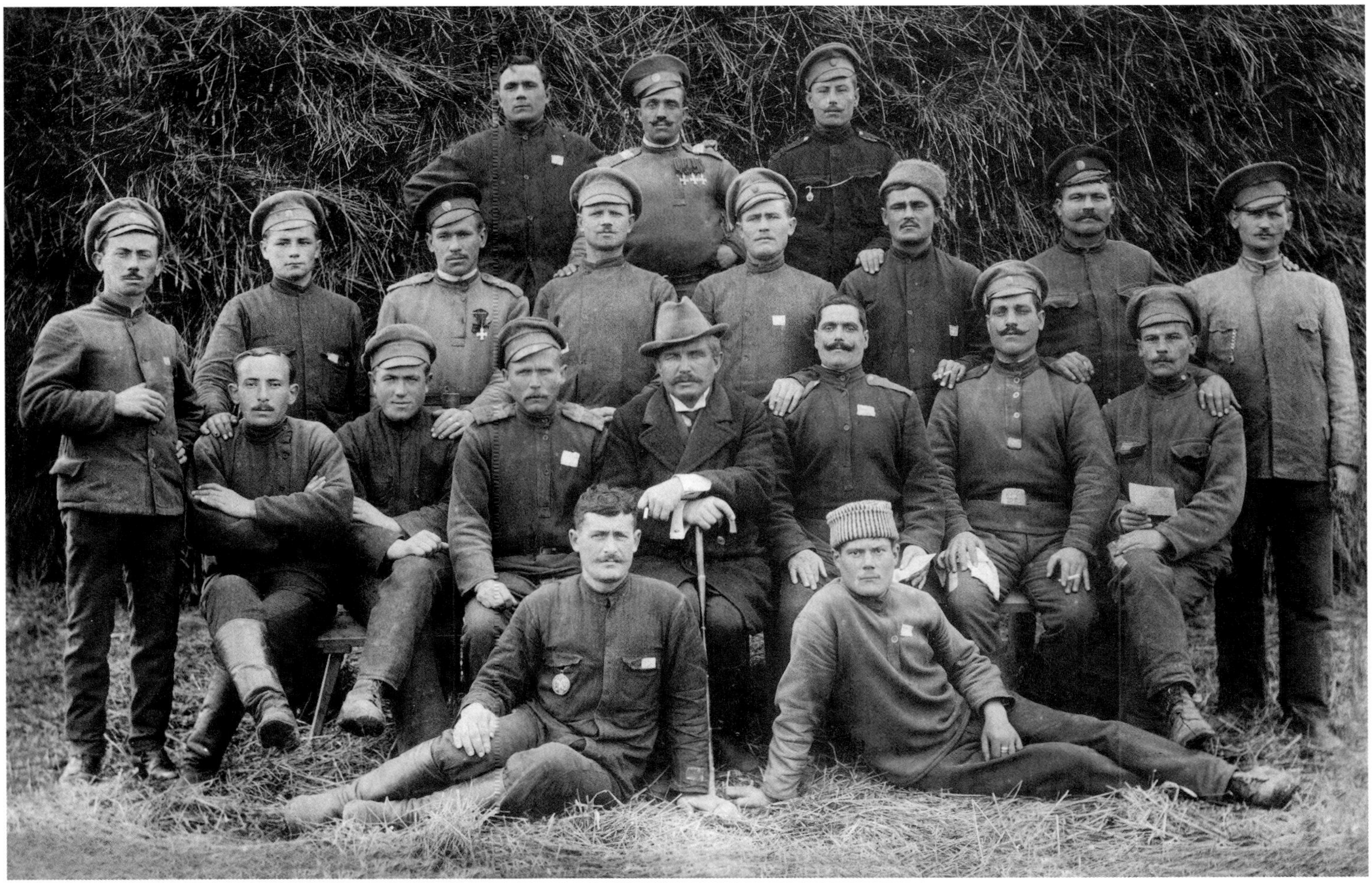

Above: The bearded officer seated in the center of the second row wears a gilded and enameled Order of St. Vladimir (Orden Svjatoi Vladimira) with swords. This decoration was instituted by Empress Catherine I in 1783. The soldier seated on the ground near the officer has been awarded the St. George Cross (Svjatoi Georggi Orden) for valor. Below: The officer on the left has been awarded the St. George Cross (Svjatoi Georggi Orden) for valor, and has fastened it to his kitel (officer tunic). Hanging on the paneled wall in the background on either side of the clock are pictures of the Czarina and the Czar.

This soldier is from the No. 289 Korotojakski Infantry Regiment, as the metal numbers on his pogoni (shoulder boards) indicate. He has an orange and black striped ribbon stitched to the button flap of his gymnastiorka (field blouse), indicating he has been awarded the St. George Cross (Svjatoi Georggi Orden) for valor

The mustached NCO in this 1915 vintage studio photo wears a gray papaha (astrakhan or fleece/fur winter cap) and carries an M1881 saber. He has two classes of the St. George Cross (Svjatoi Georggi Orden) for valor and a Czar Nicholas II medal for valor pinned to his shinel (wool overcoat).

These three NCOs have two classes of the St. George Cross (Svjatoi Georggi Orden) for valor pinned to their gymnastiorki (field blouses). Front sjéwerny (Northern front), 1916.

The NCO in this studio photo wears a Latvian Rifleman badge and has been awarded the St. George Cross (Svjatoi Georggi Orden) for valor. The braided cloth piping outlining his wool pogoni (shoulder boards) was characteristic for volunteers. Riga, Latvia (Baltic State/Country), 1917.

The NCO featured in this 1915 vintage studio photo has been awarded two classes of the St. George Cross (Svjatoi Georggi Orden) for valor in addition to three other Romanov medals.

The bearded officer in this pre- to early-war vintage cabinet portrait wears an enameled and gilded Order of St. Anne, or Svjatoi Anny Orden (barely visible under his beard), and an enameled and gilded Order of St. Stanislaus, or Svjatoi Stanislava Orden (partially hidden by his button flap). In addition, he wears various Romanov medals, as well as school/academy badges.

The NCO in this pre- to early-war vintage cabinet portrait has various grades and manufactures of marksmen badges fastened near the piped button flap of his double-breasted dark green wool tunic.

Opposite: This group of frontoviki (frontline troops) are clad in papahi (astrakhan or fleece/fur winter cap) and shineli (wool overcoats). In addition to other Romanov medals, many of these frontoviki have been awarded various classes of the St. George Cross (Svjatoi Georggi Orden) for valor. Winter 1916.

This group of frontoviki (frontline troops) pauses for a photo. The frontovik (frontline soldier) in the first row in the right corner has been awarded three classes of the St. George Cross (Svjatoi Georggi Orden) for valor.

Chapter Twenty

Late War/Independence War/ Revolution

This group photo displays a variety of headdress and overcoats. Several of the men in this photo are from armored car units as their metal caps and stitched sleeve insignia indicates. The winter of 1918.

Young revolutionaries pose for a studio photo with a bronze statue of Lenin on the table. Moscow 1918.

The winter of 1918.

Above: Many of the soldiers seen in this group photo are armed with M1891 Mosin-Nagant rifles. Baltic Independence Wars.

Left: The naval aviator in this studio photo wears a dark wool tunic with brass buttons bearing an anchor motif. The stitched insignia on his left sleeve consists of a winged propeller with two crossed swords, and a red star in the center of the crossed swords.

A group photo of early Red Army troops. The soldiers lying on the ground are holding a British manufactured Lewis machinegun.

These mounted troops are armed with M1881 sabers. The Baltic Independence War.

The soldier in this studio photo has a metal skull and crossbones fastened to his wool cap. The skull and crossbones motif was preferred by soldiers in "Shock" Battalions. Tallinn, Estonia (Baltic State/Country), during the Baltic Independence War.

These Red Army troops are armed with Mosin-Nagant rifles and an M1905 Maxim machinegun mounted on a two-wheel Sokolov carriage, 1918.

This photo, taken in Estonia during the Baltic Independence War, displays the various models of machineguns used, such as the Danish manufactured Madsen, French manufactured Hotchkiss, British manufactured Lewis and Vickers, and the M1905 Maxim.

Estonian aviators during the Baltic Independence War.

An extraordinary late war to revolutionary period photo of troops and vehicles! On the right is a twin turreted armored car, with each turret carrying an M1905 Maxim machinegun. The skull and crossbones motif, such as the one painted on the banner on the left, was preferred by "assault" or "shock" units.

Late war studio photo of the crew of a Model 1905 Maxim machinegun.

Chapter Twenty-One

Czar Nicholas II

Three Hundred Years of Romanov Dynasty.

Czar Nicholas II and Family.

Czar Nicholas II and his Generals.

Czarina Alexandra

Czar Nicholas II

Czar Nicholas II, and Czar Nicholas II and his son, the Czarevich Alexis.

Color Gallery

Issue furashka (visor cap/field cap) for enlisted rank soldiers.

Furashka (visor cap/field cap) NCOs and officers.

Dragoon helmet for enlisted ranks.

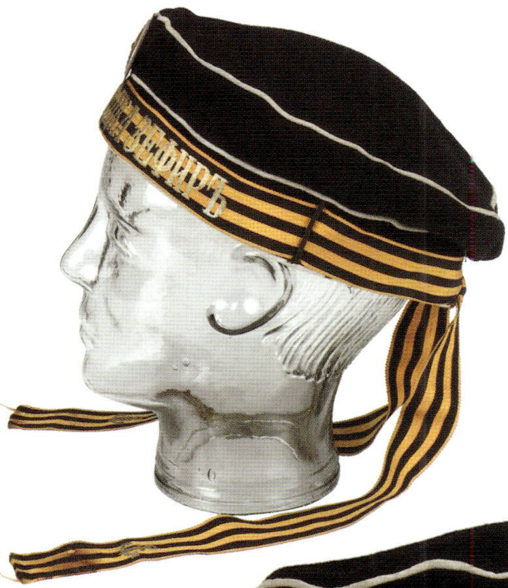

Navy cap from the ship the "Zephyr" (The West Wind).

Navy cap band from the "Gvardeiskif Ekipag."

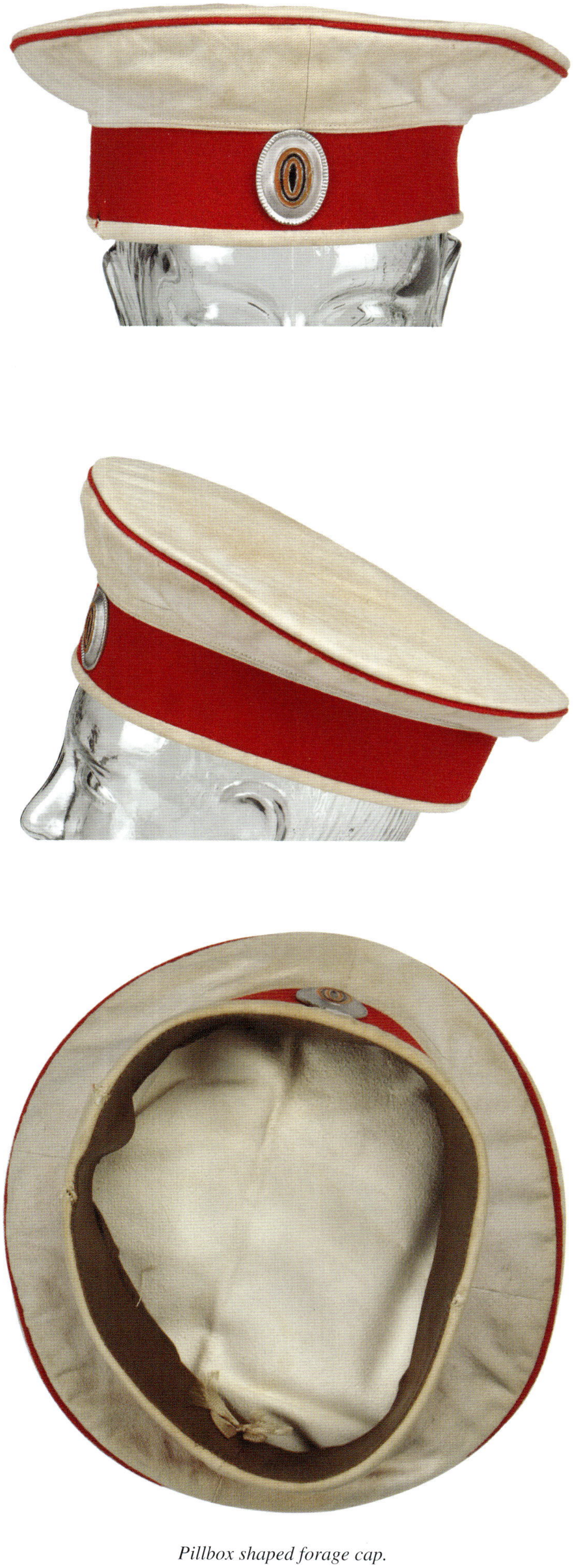

Pillbox shaped forage cap.

Summer weight visor cap with gilded Romanov double-headed eagle and porcelain cockade.

Papaha (astrakhan or fleece/fur cap).

No.176 Perewolotschenski Infantry Regiment (5 1/2 x 2 1/2 inches or 14.5 x 6.5 cm).
No.151 Pjatigorski Infantry Regiment (6 x 2 inches or 15 x 5 cm).
No. 244 Krasnostawski Infantry Regiment (5 1/2 x 2 1/2 inches or 14.5 x 6.5 cm).
No. 137 Njeshinski Infantry Regiment (6 x 2 inches or 15 x 5 cm).
No. 243 Cholmski Infantry Regiment (7 x 2 inches or 17 x 5 cm).
No. 173 Kamenezki Infantry Regiment (5 1/2 x 2 1/2 inches or 14.5 x 6.5 cm).
Unmarked shoulder board (5 1/2 x 2 1/2 inches or 14.5 x 6.5 cm).
No. 90 Oneshski Infantry Regiment (6 x 2 inches, or 15 x 5 cm).
No.139 Morschanski Infantry Regiment (6 1/2 x 2 1/2 inches or 15.5 x 5.5 cm).

Leather ammo pouches.

Forward and reverse views of brass belt buckles for artillerists (crossed cannons) and infantry.

Various shapes, sizes, and models of cockades.

Porcelain cockade.

Gilded Romanov double headed eagle.

Identification Tags.

Handmade P.O.W. (prisoner of war) trench art jewelry.

Forward and reverse views of button designs for military and civil service.

Forward and reverse view of a button design preferred by officers, NCOs, and high ranking civil servants.

Forward and reverse view of a navy button design.

Marksmen badges.

Forward and Reverse views of two Romanov medals.

Infantry krushka, or copper mess pot. Battlefield dug.

Infantry krushka, or copper mess kit stamps.

Infantry krushka with pigskin strap.

Infantry krushka stamps

Above: Infantry krushka (copper mess tin) with P.O.W. artwork and engravings.

Left: Stamps

Below: Krushka for cavalry or mounted troops.

Hand carved wood portrait of a Russian P.O.W. by Tyrolean artist Mich. Gosslitter.

Hand carved wood P.O.W. trench art jewelry or keepsake boxes. Below: Hand carved wood P.O.W. trench art cigarette case.

Handmade P.O.W. trench art made from a M1902 Putilov 7.62cm shell casing that was later nickel plated.

Forward and reverse views of the first production model steel badge for the Adrian style steel helmet (horizon blue) and the second production model steel badge for the Adrian style steel helmet (brown).

Below: Wool covered aluminum canteen. Markings are located at the neck of the canteen.

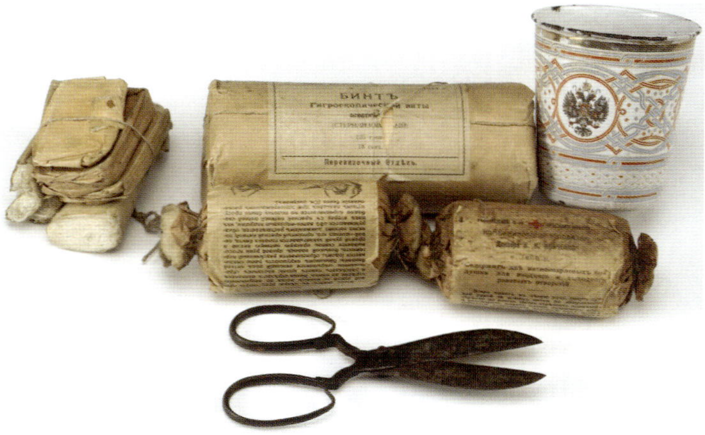

Medical bandages from the Imperial Russian Red Cross.

Leather boots (sapogi) worn by all ranks when available.

Foreign manufactured field telephone.

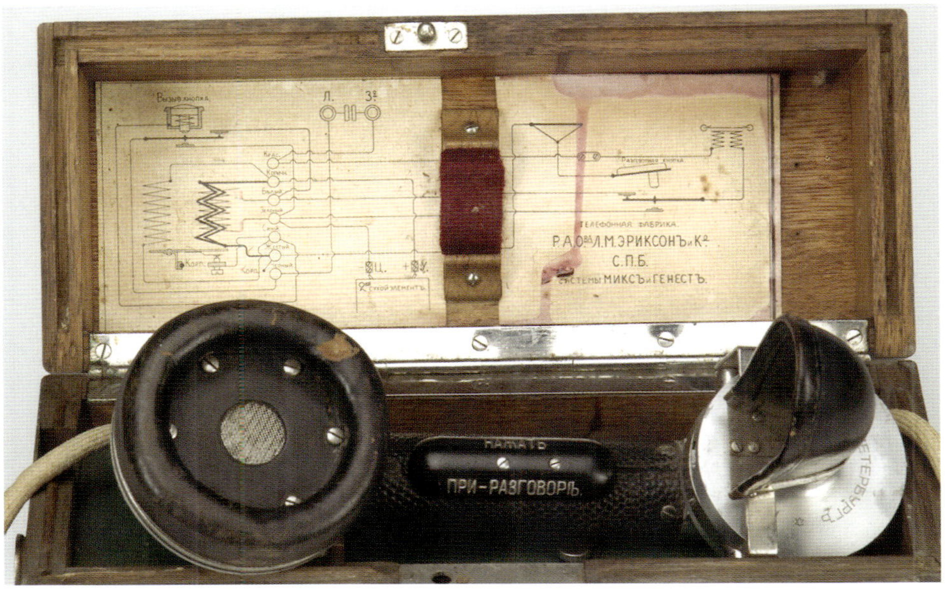

Depot stamped shelter half.

Above: Patriotic postcard depicting Mingrelian Irregular armed with kinjal (long double-edged knife) and shaska (saber). Above left: Patriotic postcard depicting a highly decorated Caucasian soldier armed with a flintlock pistol, kinjal (long double-edged knife), and shaska (saber). Above right: Patriotic postcard depicting Mingrelian Irregular armed with kinjal (long double-edged knife) and shaska (saber). Left: Patriotic postcard depicting a Caucasian irregular armed with a kinjal (long double-edged knife).

Patriotic postcard produced by the Imperial Russian Red Cross depicting a group of Cossacks enjoying the company of their comrades.

Right: Patriotic postcard depicting hungry soldiers wearing furashki (visor caps) and gymnastiorki (field blouses) standing in line holding their krushki (copper mess kits) and waiting to receive a meal from a field kitchen. Below left: Patriotic postcard produced by the Imperial Russian Red Cross depicting soldiers in wool overcoats (shineli) kneeling in the snow to receive a blessing before battle. Below right: Patriotic postcard depicting the Russian soldier in 1916 fearlessly charging into battle.

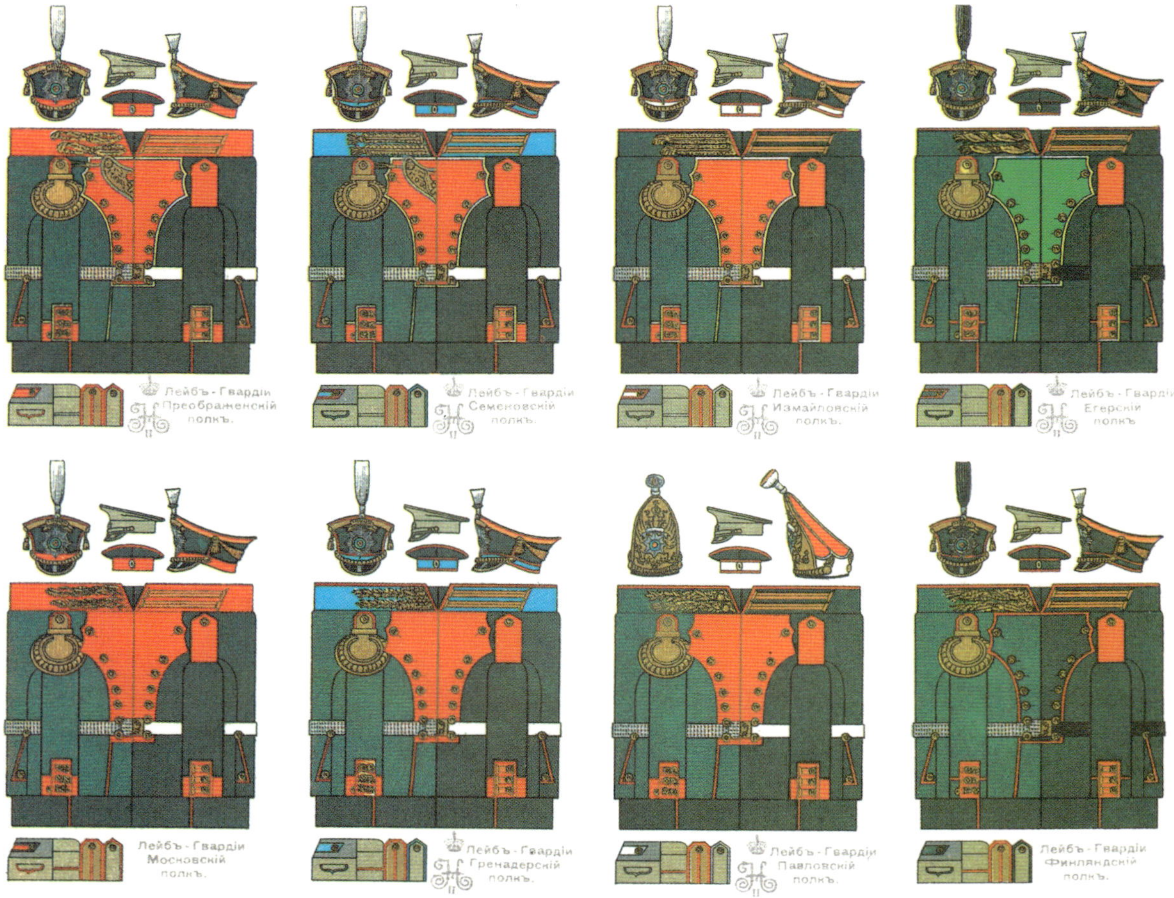

Color uniform plates by V.E. Schenk, 1910.

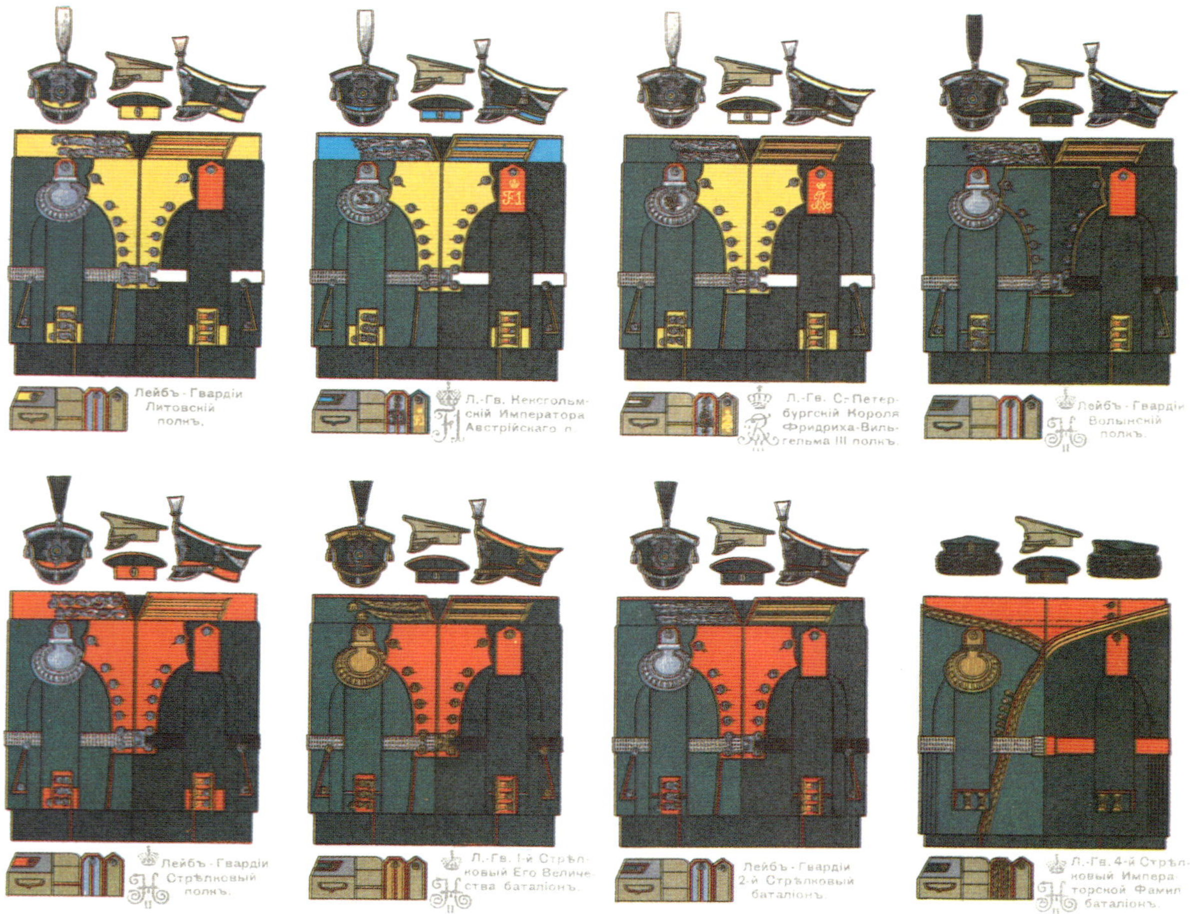

Лейбъ-Гвардіи Драгунскій полкъ.
Лейбъ-Гвардіи Конно-Гренадерскій полкъ.
Л.-Гв. Уланскій Ея В. Г. И. Александры Өеодоровны полкъ.
Л.-Гв. Улан Его Величе полкъ.
Л.-Гв. Гусарскій Его Величества полкъ.
Л.-Гв. Гродненскій Гусарскій полкъ.
Гвардейскій Запасной Кавалерійскій полкъ.
Гвардейскій Полевой Жандармскій эскадронъ.
Собственный Его Императ. Величества Конвой.
Праздничная форма офицеровъ полковъ: Кавалергардскаго и Коннаго.
Обыкновенная форма.
Л.-Гв. Казачій Его Величества полкъ.
Е. И. В. Насл. Цесарев. полкъ.
Парадная форма.
Обыкновенная форма.
Парадная форма.
Обыкновенная форма.

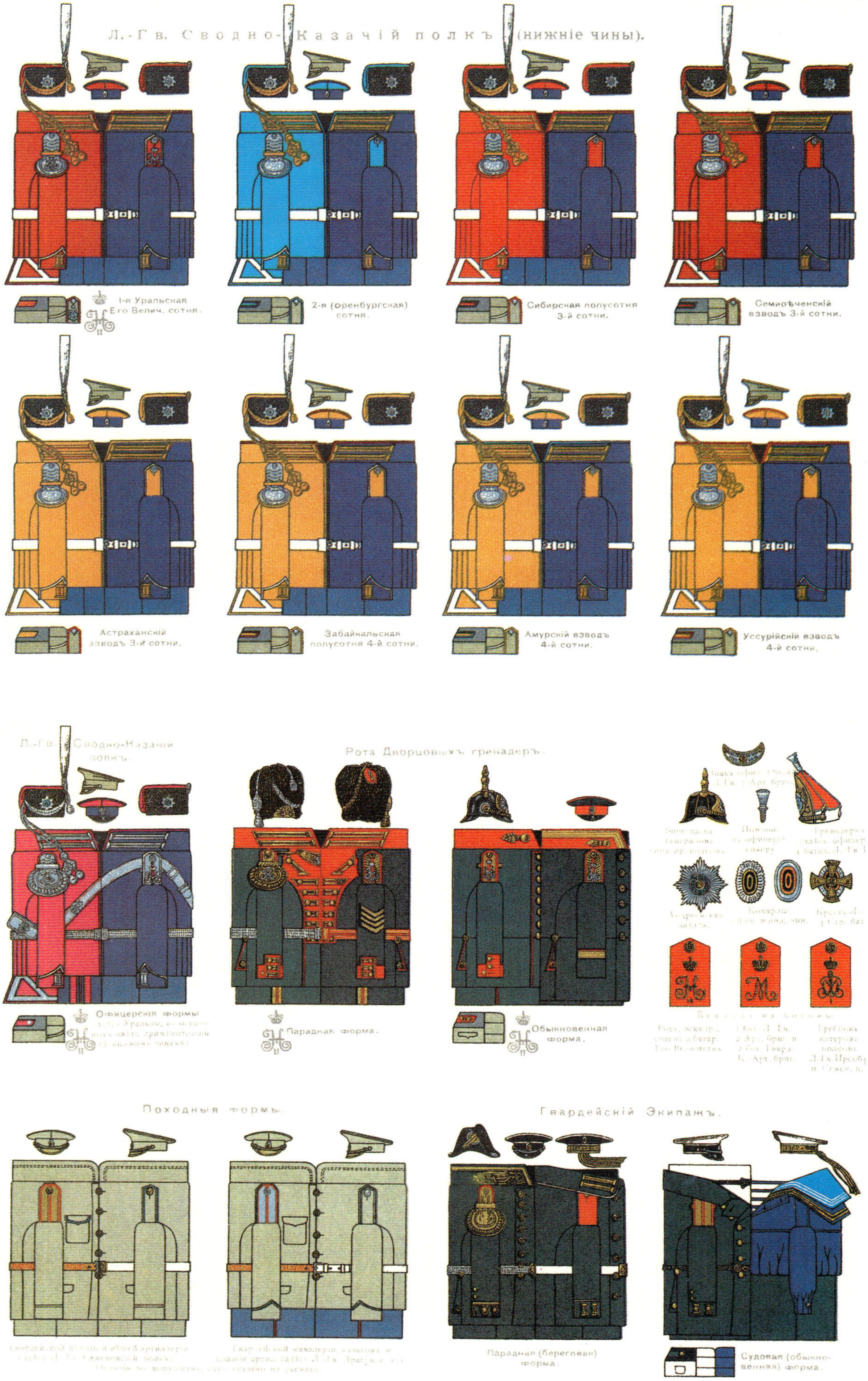
Л.-Гв. Сводно-Казачій полкъ (нижніе чины).
1-я Уральская Его Велич. сотня.
2-я (оренбургская) сотня.
Сибирская полусотня 3-й сотни.
Семирѣченскій взводъ 3-й сотни.
Астраханскій взводъ 3-й сотни.
Забайкальская полусотня 4-й сотни.
Амурскій взводъ 4-й сотни.
Уссурійскій взводъ 4-й сотни.
Рота Дворцовыхъ гренадеръ.
Офицерскія формы
Парадная форма.
Обыкновенная форма.
Походныя формы.
Гвардейскій Экипажъ.
Парадная (береговая) форма.
Судовая (обыкновенная) форма.

1-й Лейбъ-Гренадерскій Екатеринославскій Имп. Александра II п.
2-й Гр. Ростовскій Е. И. В. В. Кн. Михаила Александровича полкъ.
3-й Гр. Перновскій Короля Фридриха-Вильгельма IV полкъ.
4-й Гр. Несвижскій Г.-Фельдм. Кн. Барклая-де-Толли полкъ.
5-й Грен. Кіевскій Г.-Ф. Кн. Николая Репнина, нынѣ Ея И.В.В.Кн. Елисаветы Θеодоровны п.
6-й Гр. Таврическій Ген. Фельдм. В.Кн. Михаила Николаевича полкъ
7-й Гр. Самогитскій Ген.-Адъют. Графа Тотлебена полкъ.
8-й Гр. Московскій Вел. Герцога Мекленбургъ-Шверинскаго Фридриха п.
9-й Гр. Сибирскій Ген.-Фельдм. В. Кн. Николая Николаевича п.
10-й Гр. Малороссійскій Г.-Ф. Гр. Румянцева-Задунайскаго полкъ.
11-й Гр. Фанагорійскій Генералис. Кн. Суворова, нынѣ Е. И.В.В.Кн. Димитрія Павловича п.
12-й Гр. Астраханскій Импер. Александра III полкъ.
13-й Лейбъ-Грен. Эриванскій Его Величества п.
14-й Гренадер. Грузинскій Ген. Котляревскаго полкъ.
15-й Гр. Тифлисскій Е. И. В. В. Кн. Константина Константиновича п.
16-й Гр. Мингрельскій Е. И. В. В. Кн. Димитрія Константиновича полкъ.

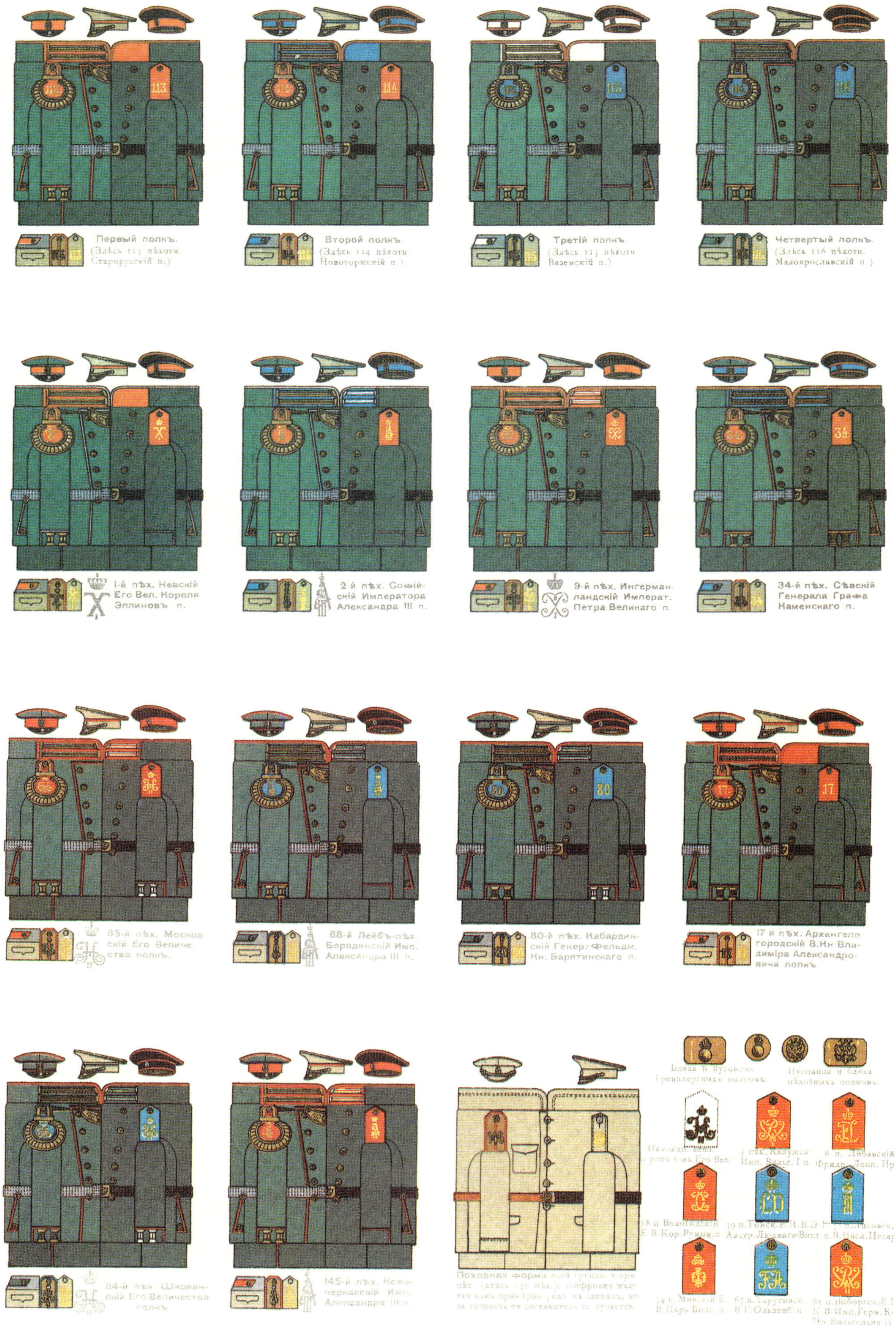
Первый полкъ.
(Здѣсь 113 пѣхотн. Старорусскій п.)
Второй полкъ.
(Здѣсь 114 пѣхотн. Новоторжскій п.)
Третій полкъ
(Здѣсь 115 пѣхотн. Вяземскій п.)
Четвертый полкъ.
(Здѣсь 116 пѣхотн. Малоярославскій п.)
1-й пѣх. Невскій Его Вел. Короля Эллиновъ п.
2-й пѣх. Софійскій Императора Александра III п.
9-й пѣх. Ингерманландскій Императ. Петра Великаго п.
34-й пѣх. Сѣвскій Генерала Графа Каменскаго п.
65-й пѣх. Московскій Его Величества полкъ.
68-й Лейбъ-пѣх. Бородинскій Имп. Александра III п.
80-й пѣх. Кабардинскій Генер.-Фельдм. Кн. Барятинскаго п.
17 й пѣх. Архангелогородскій В.Кн. Владиміра Александровича полкъ
84-й пѣх. Ширванскій Его Величества полкъ
145-й пѣх. Новочеркасскій Имп. Александра III п.
Бляха и пуговица Гренадерскихъ полковъ.
Пуговица и бляха пѣхотныхъ полковъ.

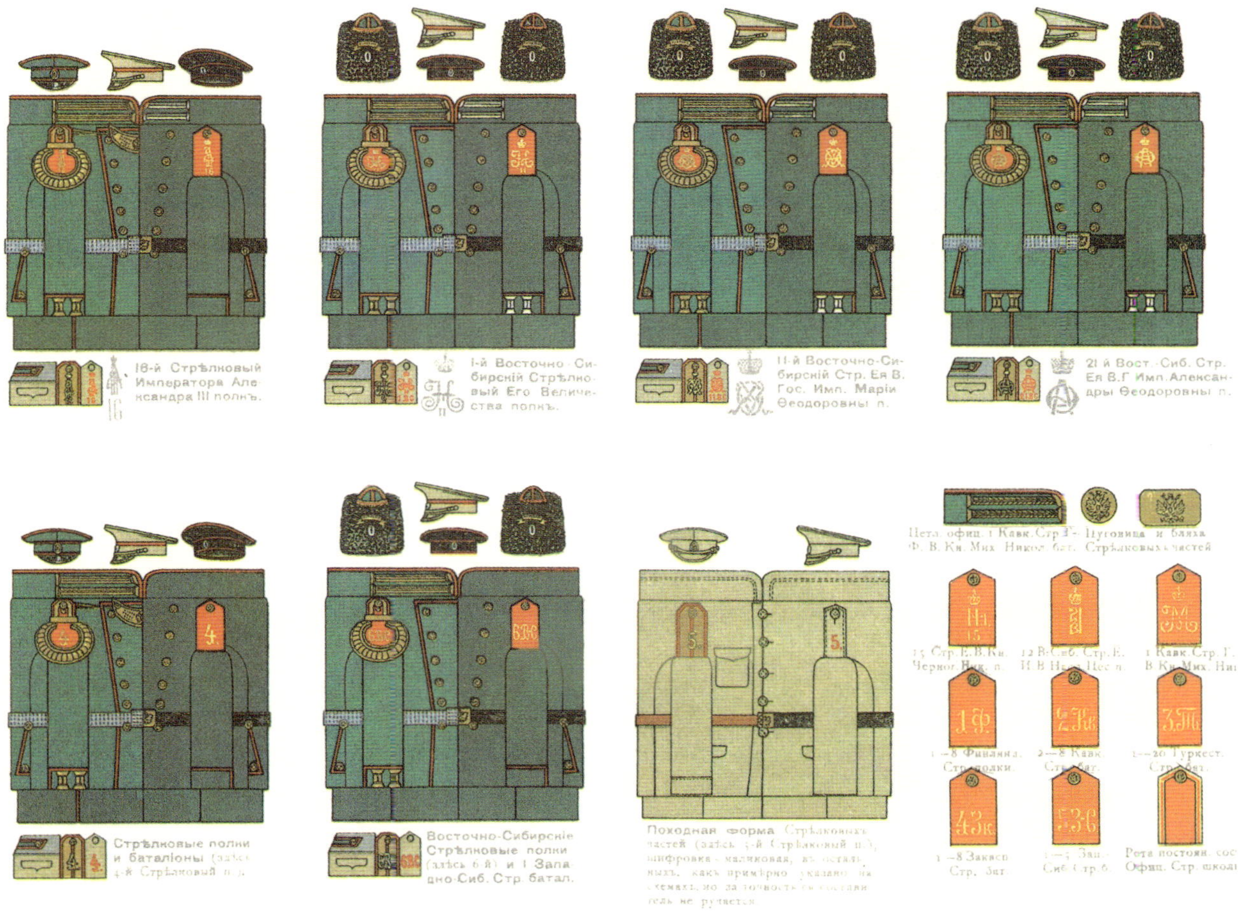
16-й Стрѣлковый Императора Александра III полкъ.
1-й Восточно-Сибирскій Стрѣлковый Его Величества полкъ.
11-й Восточно-Сибирскій Стр. Ея В. Гос. Имп. Маріи Θеодоровны п.
21 й Вост.-Сиб. Стр. Ея В.Г Имп. Александры Θеодоровны п.
Стрѣлковые полки и баталіоны
Восточно-Сибирскіе Стрѣлковые полки (здѣсь 6-й) и 1 Западно-Сиб. Стр. батал.
Походная форма
Пуговица и бляха Стрѣлковыхъ частей

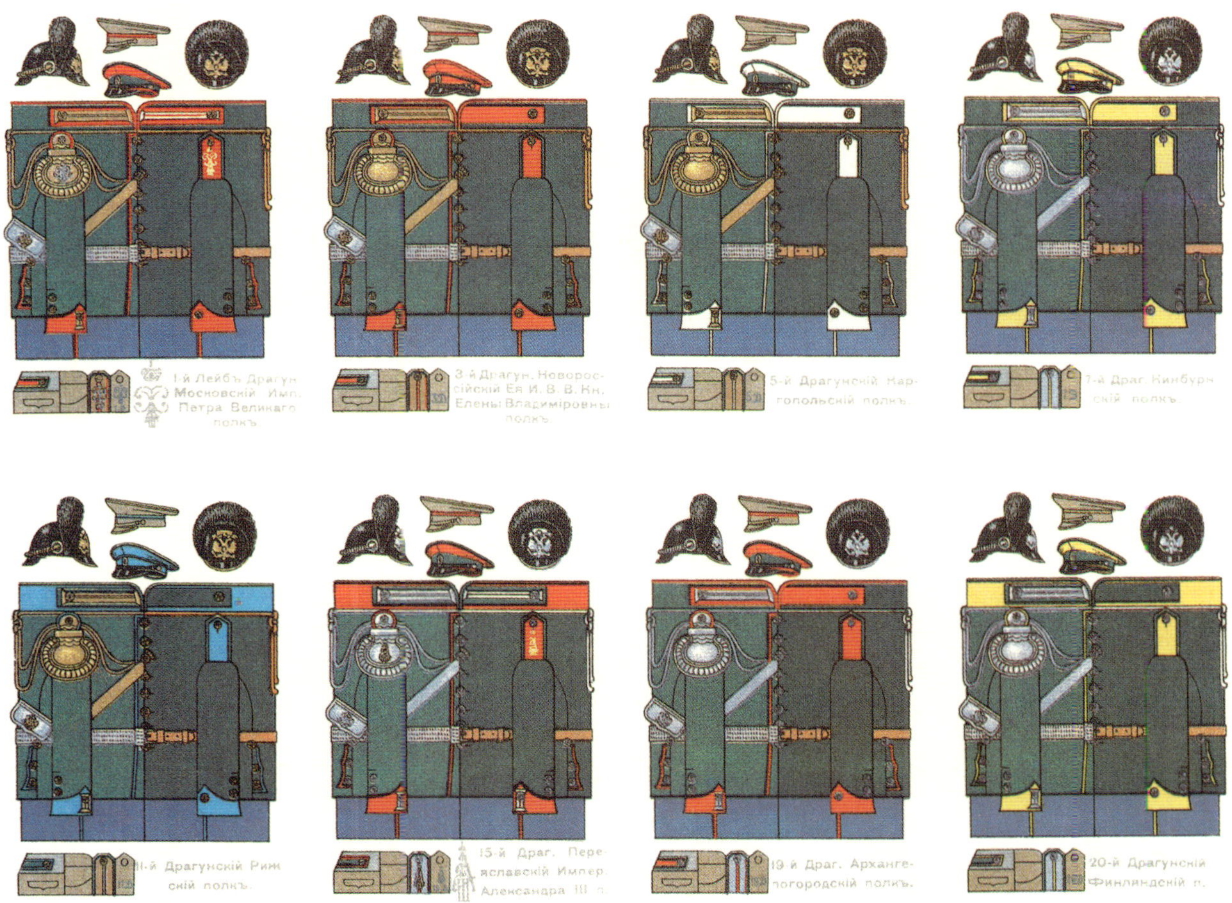
1-й Лейбъ Драгун. Московскій Имп. Петра Великаго полкъ.
3-й Драгун. Новороссійскій Ея И. В. В. Кн. Елены Владиміровны полкъ.
5-й Драгунскій Каргопольскій полкъ.
7-й Драг. Кинбурнскій полкъ.
11-й Драгунскій Рижскій полкъ.
15-й Драг. Переяславскій Императора Александра III п.
19 й Драг. Архангелогородскій полкъ.
20-й Драгунскій Финляндскій п.

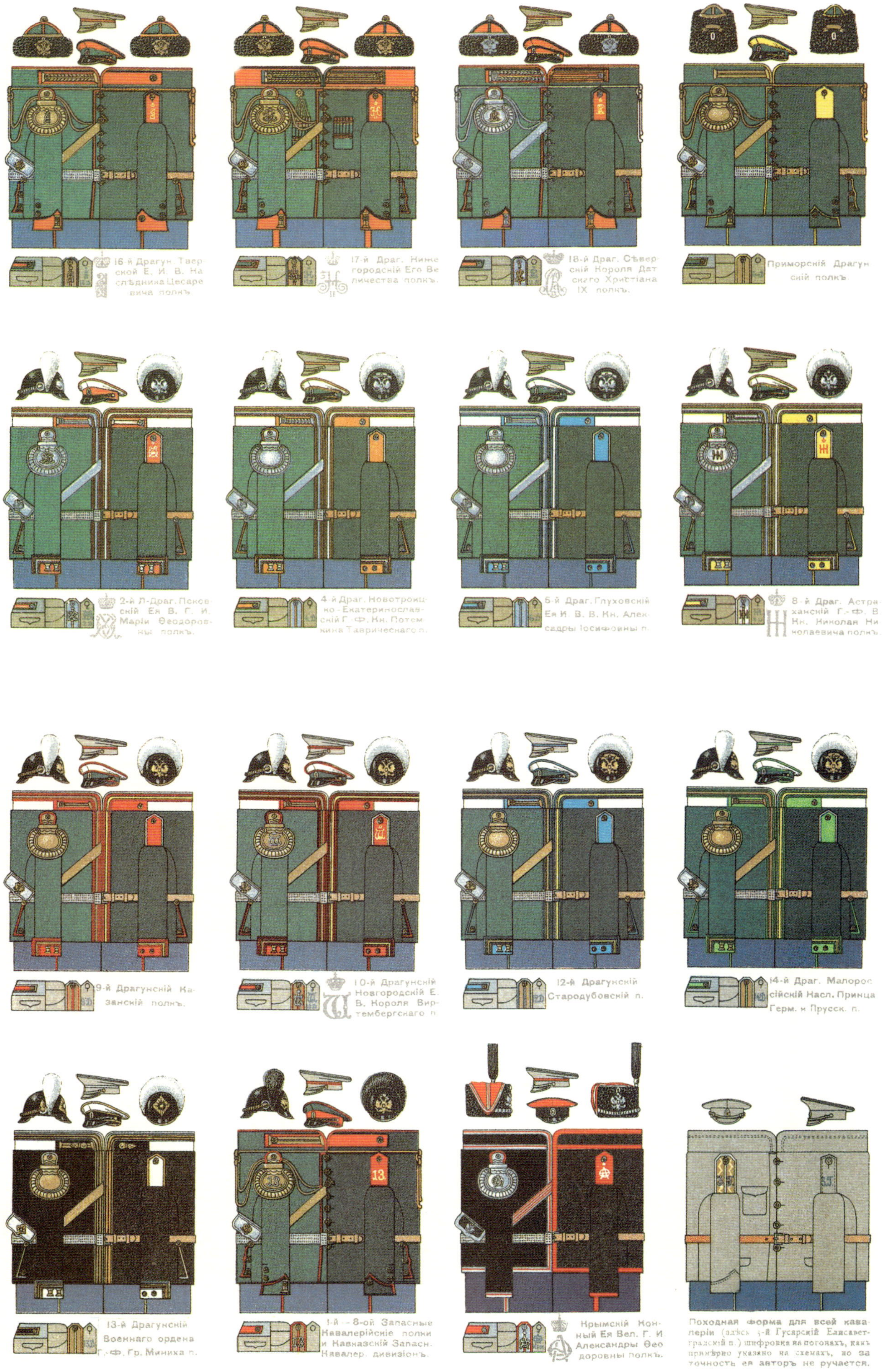
16-й Драгун. Тверской Е. И. В. Наслѣдника Цесаревича полкъ
17-й Драг. Нижегородскій Его Величества полкъ.
18-й Драг. Сѣверскій Короля Датскаго Христіана IX полкъ.
Приморскій Драгунскій полкъ
2-й Л-Драг. Псковскій Ея В. Г. И. Маріи Ѳеодоровны полкъ.
4-й Драг. Новотроицко-Екатеринославскій Г.-Ф. Кн. Потемкина Таврическаго п.
5-й Драг. Глуховскій Ея И. В. В. Кн. Александры Іосифовны п.
8-й Драг. Астраханскій Г.-Ф. В. Кн. Николая Николаевича полкъ.
9-й Драгунскій Казанскій полкъ.
10-й Драгунскій Новгородскій Е. В. Короля Виртембергскаго п.
12-й Драгунскій Стародубовскій п.
14-й Драг. Малороссійскій Насл. Принца Герм. и Прусск. п.
13-й Драгунскій Военнаго ордена Г.-Ф. Гр. Миниха п.
1-й -- 8-ой Запасные Кавалерійскіе полки и Кавказскій Запасн. Кавалер. дивизіонъ.
Крымскій Конный Ея Вел. Г. И. Александры Ѳеодоровны полкъ.
Походная форма для всей кавалеріи (здѣсь 5-й Гусарскій Елисаветградскій п.) шифровка на погонахъ, какъ примѣрно указано на схемахъ, но за точность ея авторъ не ручается.

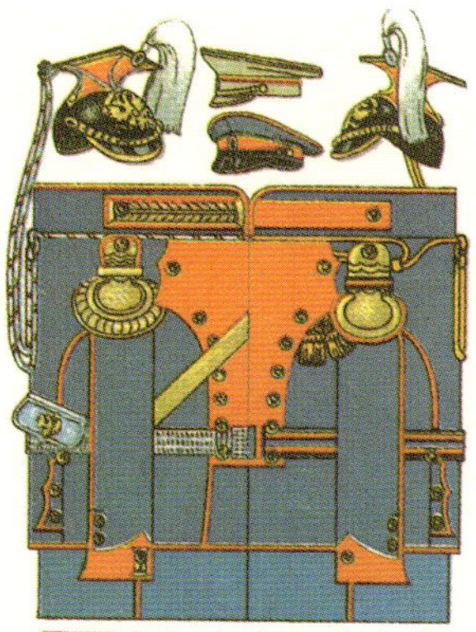
1-й Уланскій С.-Петербургскій Ген.-Ф. Князя Меншикова полкъ.

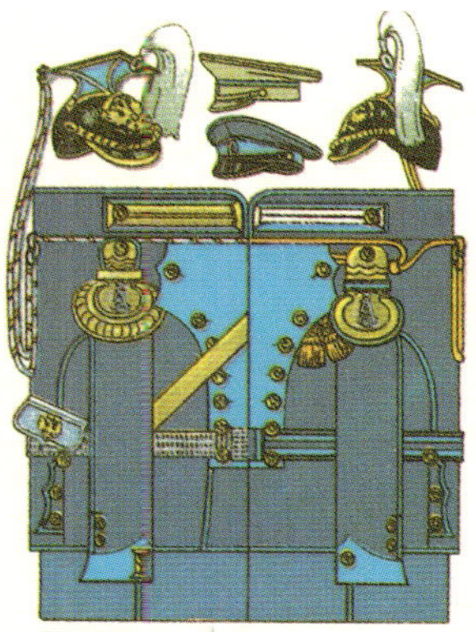
2-й Лейбъ-Уланскій Курляндскій Императора Александра III п.

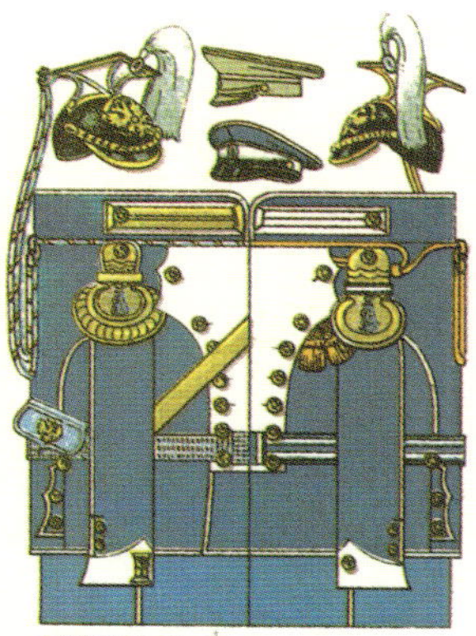
3-й Уланскій Смоленскій Имп. Александра III полкъ.

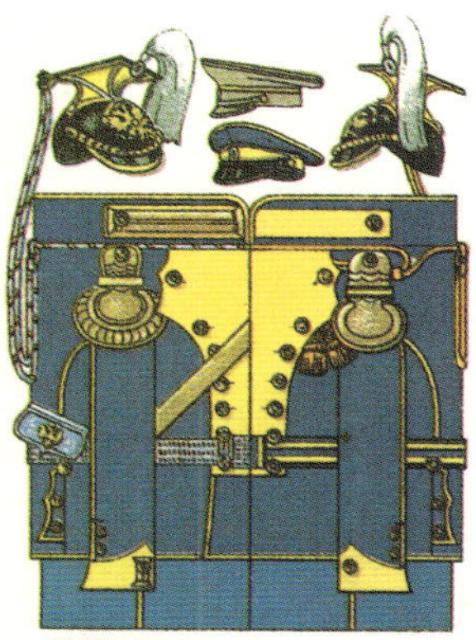
4-й Уланскій Харьковскій п.

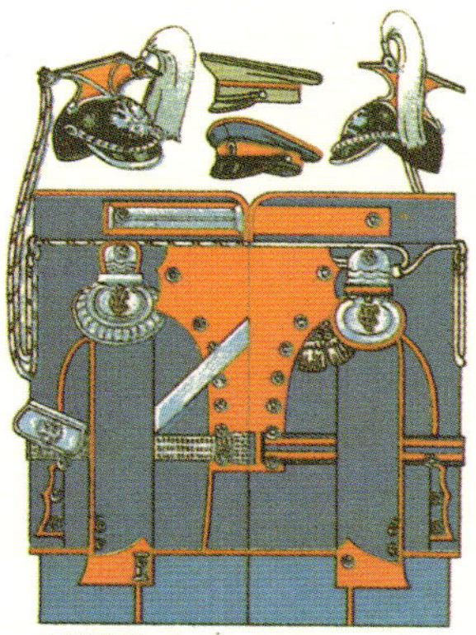
5-й Уланскій Литовскій Е. В. Короля Виктора Эммануила III п.

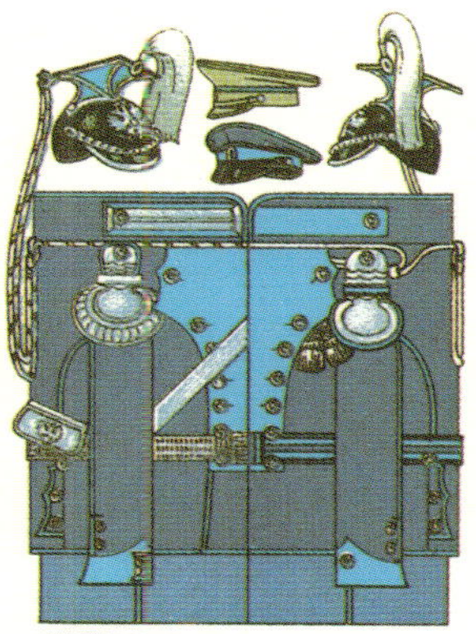
6-й Уланскій Волынскій п.

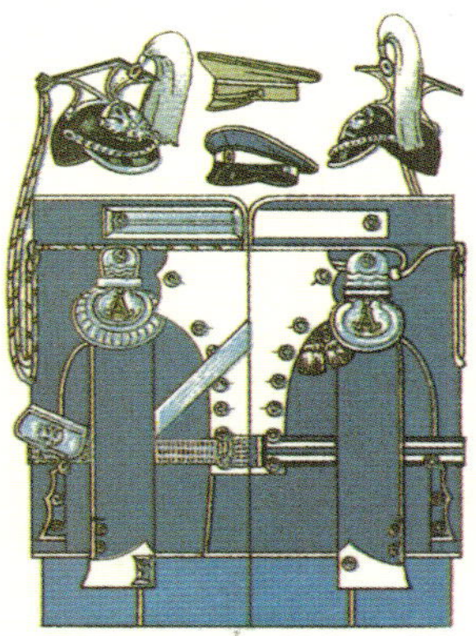
7-й Уланскій Ольвіопольскій Е. В. Короля Испанск. Альфонса XIII п.

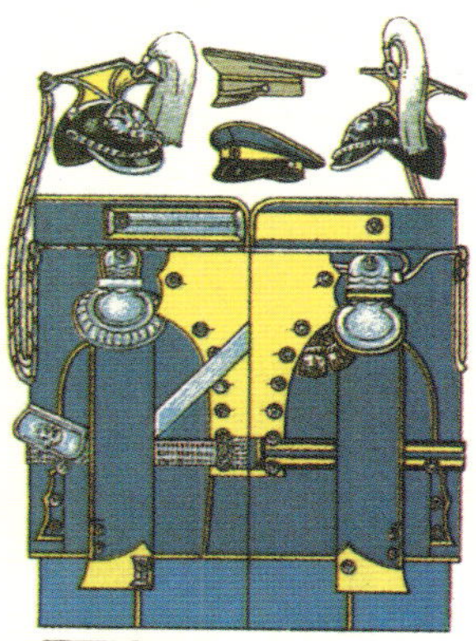
8-й Уланскій Вознесенскій п.

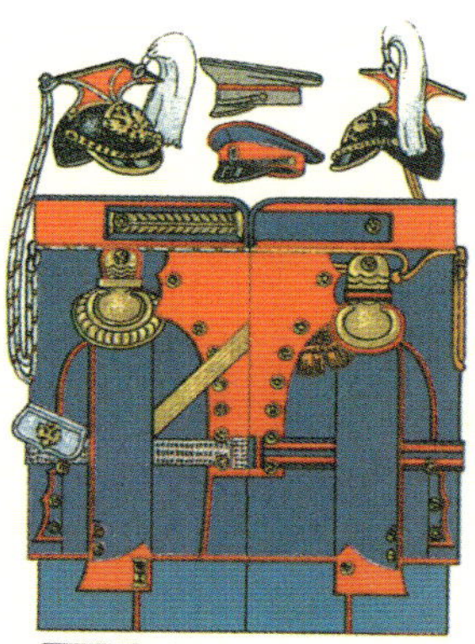
9-й Уланскій Бугскій Е.И.К.В. Э.-Г. Австрійскаго Франца Фердинанда полкъ.

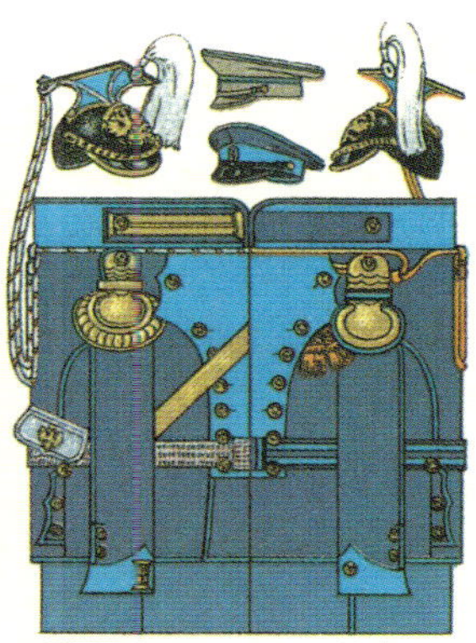
10-й Уланскій Одесскій Е. В. В. Г. Люксембургскаго и Нассаускаго полкъ.

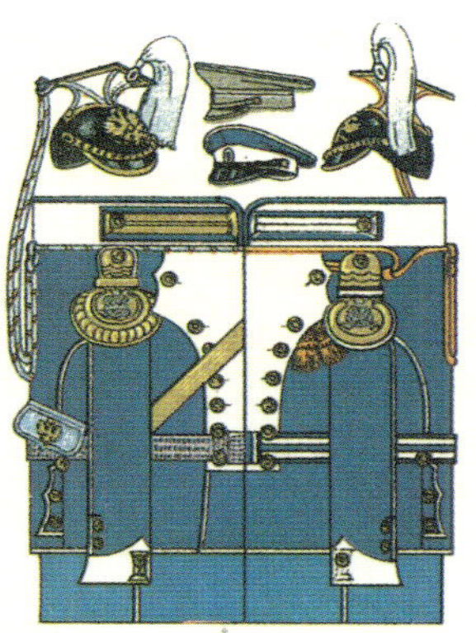
11-й Уланскій Чугуевскій Ея В. Г. И. Маріи Θеодоровны полкъ.

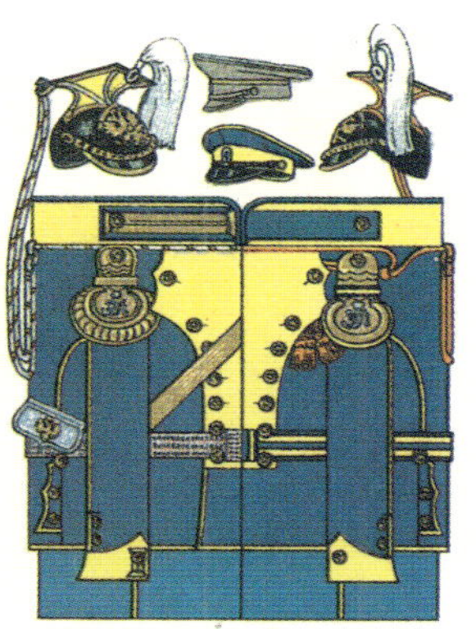
12-й Улан. Бѣлгородскій Е. В. Имп. Австр. Кор. Венгерск. Франца-Іосифа I п.

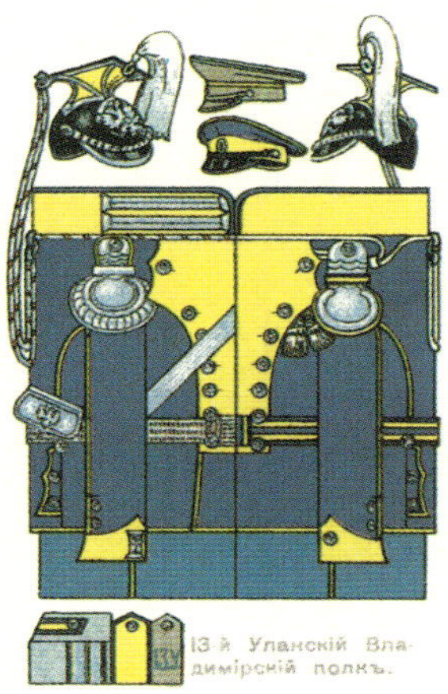
13-й Уланскій Владимірскій полкъ.

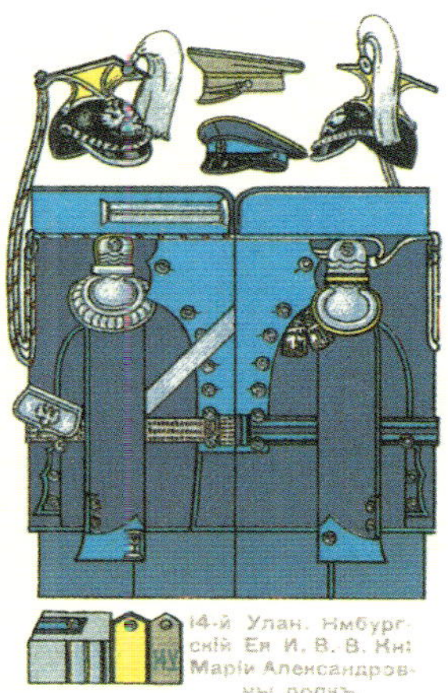
14-й Улан. Ямбургскій Ея И. В. В. Кн. Маріи Александровны полкъ.

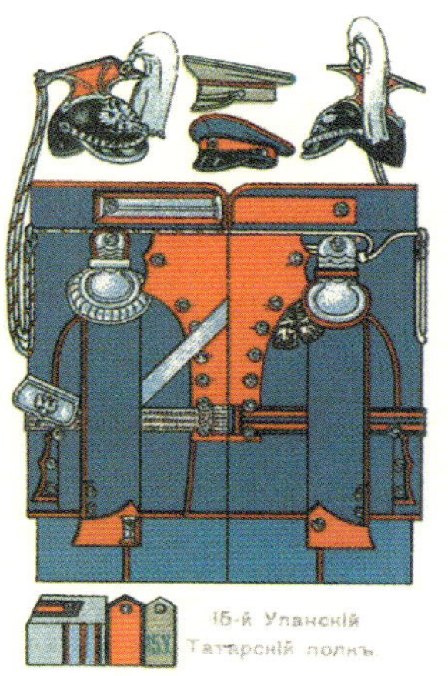
15-й Уланскій Татарскій полкъ.

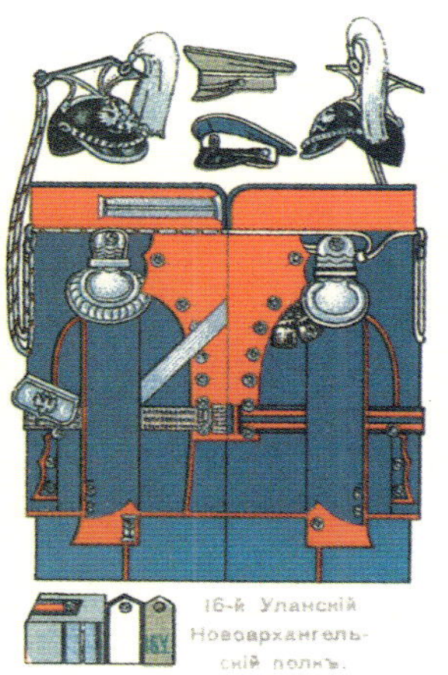
16-й Уланскій Новоархангельскій полкъ.

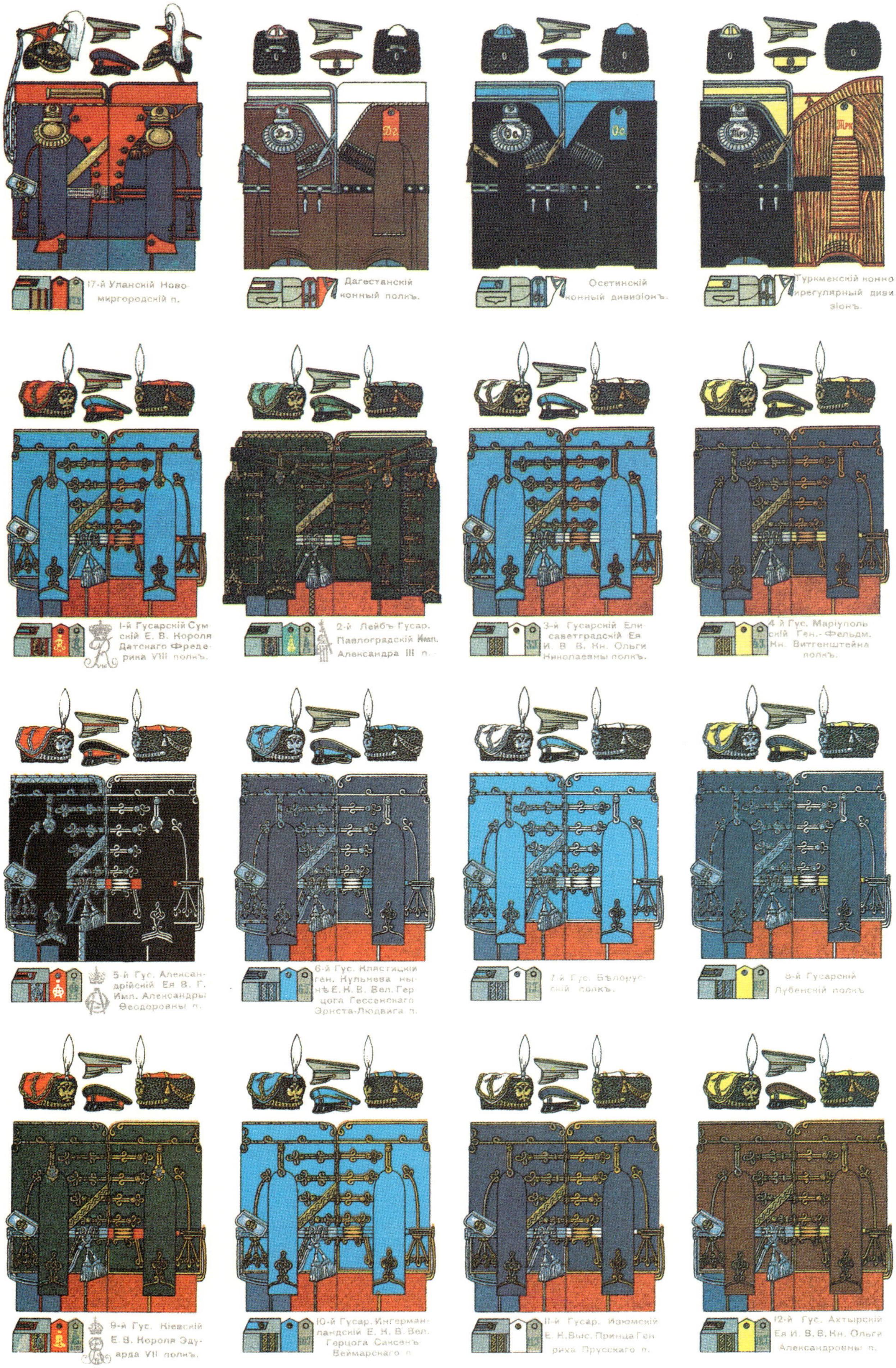
17-й Уланскій Ново-миргородскій п.
Дагестанскій конный полкъ.
Осетинскій конный дивизіонъ.
Туркменскій конно иррегулярный дивизіонъ.
1-й Гусарскій Сумскій Е. В. Короля Датскаго Фредерика VIII полкъ.
2-й Лейбъ Гусар. Павлоградскій Имп. Александра III п.
3-й Гусарскій Елисаветградскій Ея И. В. В. Кн. Ольги Николаевны полкъ.
4-й Гус. Маріупольскій Ген.-Фельдм. Кн. Витгенштейна полкъ.
5-й Гус. Александрійскій Ея В. Г. Имп. Александры Θеодоровны п.
6-й Гус. Клястицкій ген. Кульнева нынѣ Е. К. В. Вел. Герцога Гессенскаго Эрнста-Людвига п.
7-й Гус. Бѣлорусскій полкъ.
8-й Гусарскій Лубенскій полкъ.
9-й Гус. Кіевскій Е. В. Короля Эдуарда VII полкъ.
10-й Гусар. Ингерманландскій Е. К. В. Вел. Герцога Саксенъ-Веймарскаго п.
11-й Гусар. Изюмскій Е. К. Выс. Принца Генриха Прусскаго п.
12-й Гус. Ахтырскій Ея И. В. В. Кн. Ольги Александровны п.

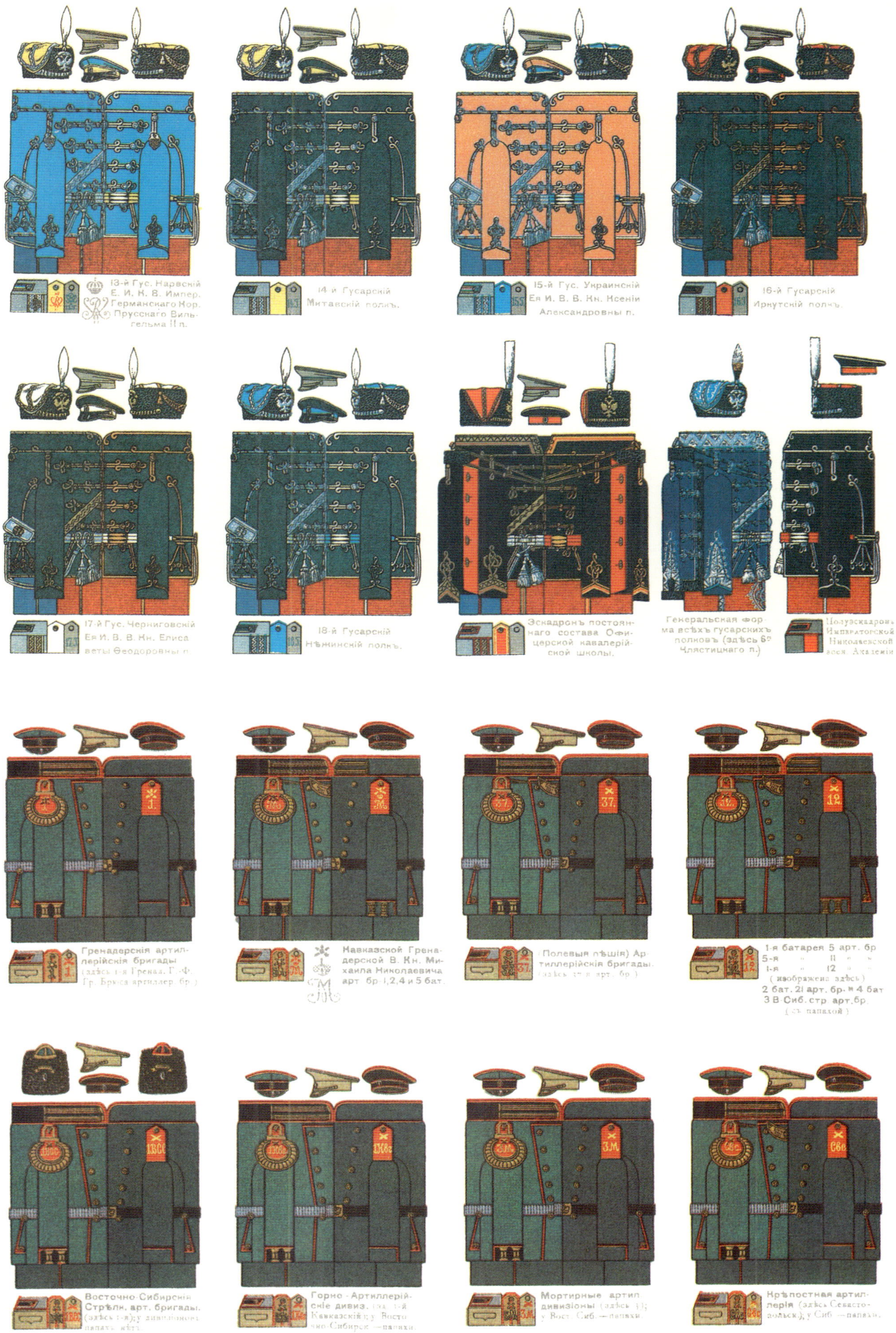
13-й Гус. Нарвскій Е. И. К. В. Импер. Германскаго Кор. Прусскаго Вильгельма II п.
14-й Гусарскій Митавскій полкъ.
15-й Гус. Украинскій Ея И. В. В. Кн. Ксеніи Александровны п.
16-й Гусарскій Иркутскій полкъ.
17-й Гус. Черниговскій Ея И. В. В. Кн. Елисаветы Өеодоровны п.
18-й Гусарскій Нѣжинскій полкъ.
Эскадронъ постояннаго состава Офицерской кавалерійской школы.
Генеральская форма всѣхъ гусарскихъ полковъ (здѣсь 6º Чпястицкаго п.)
Полуэскадронъ Императорской Николаевской воен. Академіи
Гренадерскія артиллерійскія бригады
Кавказской Гренадерской В. Кн. Михаила Николаевича арт. бр. 1, 2, 4 и 5 бат.
(Полевыя пѣшія) Артиллерійскія бригады.
1-я батарея 5 арт. бр
5-я 11
1-я 12
(изображена здѣсь)
2 бат. 21 арт. бр. и 4 бат
3 В-Сиб. стр. арт. бр.
(съ папахой)
Восточно-Сибирскія Стрѣлк. арт. бригады.
Горно-Артиллерійскіе дивиз.
Мортирные артил. дивизіоны
у Вост. Сиб. — папахи.
Крѣпостная артиллерія (здѣсь Севастопольск.); у Сиб. — папахи.

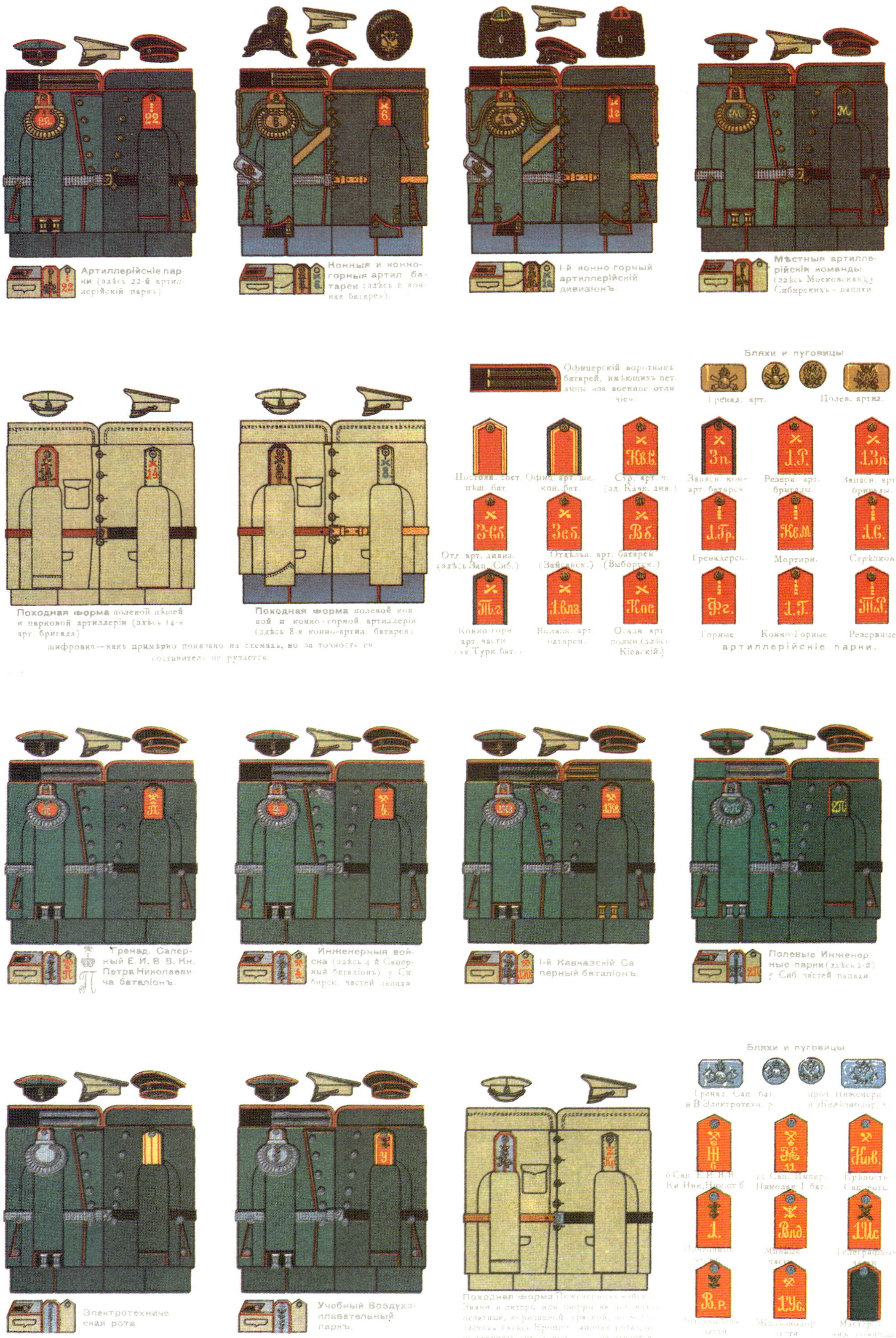
Артиллерійскіе парки
Конныя и конно-горныя артил. батареи
1-й конно-горный артиллерійскій дивизіонъ
Мѣстныя артиллерійскія команды
Бляхи и пуговицы
Походная форма
Гренадеръ
Мортирн.
Горные
Конно-Горные
Резервные
артиллерійскіе парки.
1-й Кавказскій Саперный баталіонъ.
Электротехническая рота
Учебный Воздухоплавательный паркъ.

Appendix One

Organization of the Russian Army, 1917

(This list has been translated and adapted from a list compiled by the High Command of the k.u.k (imperial and royal) or Austro-Hungarian Armed Forces in 1917)

Infantry Regiments (Pjechóta polk)
Abchasski No. 160
Achalzychski No. 162
Achtyrski No. 545
Achulginski No. 261
Akermanski No. 255
Alexandrijski No. 282
Alexandro-Newski No. 198
Alexandropolski No. 161
Alexandrowski No. 418
Alexjejewski No. 31
Anapski No. 335
Apscheronski No. 81
Archangelogorodski No. 17
Ardagano-Michailowski No. 204
Arsamasski No. 469
Aslandusski No. 186
Asowski No. 45
Atkarski No. 419
Awarski No. 187

Bachmutski No. 415
Bachtschisarajski No. 246
Bakinski No. 153
Balaschowski No. 313
Baltinski No. 250
Barnaulski No. 492
Baschkadyklarski No. 185
Baturinski No. 175
Bauski (Latvian) No. 7
Belebejewski No. 235
Benderski No. 132
Berdjanski No. 245
Beresinski No. 294
Bessarrabski No. 129
Birski No. 484
Bjelewski No. 71
Bjelezki No. 497
Bjelgorajski No. 326
Bjelgorodski No. 447
Bjelomorski No. 89
Bjeloserski No. 13
Bjelostokski No. 50
Bobrujski No. 301
Bogoduchowski No. 273
Bogorodski No. 209
Bogutscharski No. 234
Bolchowski No. 138
Borisogjebski No. 236
Borodinski No. 68
Brazlawski No. 260
Brestski No.49
Brjanski No.35
Bronizki No. 210
Bugulminski No. 319
Buguruslanski No.440
Busulukski No. 329
Butyrski No. 66

Charkowski No. 449
Chersonski No. 130
Cholmogorski No. 513
Cholmski No. 243
Chortizki No. 400
Chotinski No. 252
Chwalinski No. 316

Dagestanski No. 82
Danilowski No. 480
Dankowski No. 470
Derbentski No. 154
Dissninski No.512
Dmitrowski No. 444
Dnjeprowski No. 46
Donskoi No. 111
Dorogobushski No. 143
Drisski No. 317
Drogitschinski No. 231
Dubnenski No. 299
Dubrowski No. 487
Duchowtschinski No. 267
Dunajski No. 249
Dwinski No. 91

Estljandski No. 8

Fateshki No. 448
Feodosijski No. 134

Galizki No. 20
Gatschinski No. 270
Georgiewski No. 264
Gdowski No. 272
Glaskowski No. 333
Gluchowski No. 315
Gorbatowski No. 218
Gorijski No. 202
Grajworonski No. 237
Grasowjezki No. 296
Grochowski No. 182
Grosnenski No.262
Gshatski No. 509
Gunibski No. 263
Gurijski No. 159

Ignmenski No. 550
Ilezki No. 489
Imeretinski No.157
Ingermanljandski No. 9
Ingulski No. 500
Insarski No. 196
Irbitski No. 334
Irkutski No. 93
Isborgski No. 177
Ishorski No. 293
Isjumski No. 274
Ismailski No. 189
Iwangorodski No. 99
Jakutski No. 42
Jamburgski No. 435
Jaroslawski No. 117
Jekaterinburgski No. 37
Jelanski No. 485
Jelezki No. 33
Jelisawetgradski No. 256
Jelisawetpolski No. 156
Jenissejski No. 94
Jepifanski No. 227
Jewpatorijski No. 257
Juchnowski No. 224
Jurjewiczki No. 323
Jurjewski No. 98

Kabardinski No. 80
Kadnikowski No. 479
Kajazinski No. 477
Kalushski No. 5
Kamenezki No. 173
Kamski No. 110
Kamtschatski No. 44
Kamyschinski No. 404
Karatschewski No. 401
Kargopolski No. 425
Karsski No. 188
Kasanski No. 64
Kaschinski No. 442
Kaschirski No.144
Kaspijski No. 148
Kawkaski No. 737

Kertsch-Jenikolski No. 135
Kinburnski No. 467
Kirsanowski No. 286
Kischewski No. 258
Klinski No. 493
Kljasminski No. 324
Kobrinski No. 171
Kodnikowski No. 479
Kologrinski No. 712
Kolomenski No. 119
Kolpinski No. 422
Kolywanski No. 40
Konstaninogradski No. 239
Koporski No. 4
Korotojakski No. 289
Korotschanski No. 457
Korsunski No. 327
Koselski No. 471
Koslowski No. 123
Kostromskoi No. 19
Kotelnitscheski No. 219
Kowelski No. 297
Kowenski No. 495
Kowrowski No. 217
Krasninski No. 222
Krasnocholmski No. 463
Krasnojarski No. 95
Krasnoselski No. 271
Krasnostawski No. 244
Kremenezki No. 311
Kremetschugski No. 32
Kremlewski No. 214
Krolewetzki No. 452
Kromski No. 278
Kronschlotski No. 200
Kronschtadski No. 199
Krymski No. 73
Kubanski No. 76
Kubinski No. 155
Kulikowski No. 288
Kupjanski No. 276
Kurinski No. 79
Kursemski No. 3 (Latvian)
Kurski No. 125
Kusnezki No. 408
Kutaiski No. 158

Ladoshski No. 16
Laishewski No. 305
Largo-Kagulski N0. 191
Lebedinski No. 275
Lenkoransko-Nascheburgski No. 163
Lepelski No. 542
Lgowski No. 405
Libawski No. 6
Lichwinski No. 537
Lidski No. 172
Litowski No.51
Livjandski No. 97
Liwenski No. 225

Ljesnoi No. 197
Ljublinski No. 59
Lockwizki No. 279
Lodeinopolski No. 428
Lorijski No. 208
Luganski No. 417
Lukowski No. 242
Lushski No. 423
Luzki No. 165

Malmyshski No. 266
Maloarchangelski No. 292
Malojaroslawski No. 116
Mariupolski No. 247
Medynski No. No. 538
Meschtschowski No. 481
Mesenski No. 516
Minski No. 54
Migorodski No. 168
Miropolski No. 459
Modlinski No. 57
Mogilewski No. 26
Mokschanski No. 306
Molodetschnenski No. 170
Morschanski No. 139
Moshaiski No. 141
Mosalski No. 472
Mstislawski No. 298
Muchawetzki No. 393
Murmanski No. 514
Muromski No. 21
Mzenski No. 285

Narymski No. 468
Narwski No. 3
Nawaginski No. 78
Neischlotski No. 87
Newski No. 1
Nikolajewski No. 254
Nikolski No. 211
Nikopolski No. 399
Nishegorodski No. 22
Nishnednjeprowski No. 398
Nisowski No. 23
Njeshinski No. 137
Nowgorod-Sjewerski No. 304
Nowgorodski No. 10
Nowobajasetski No. 207
Nowochoperski No. 409
Nowogorod-Wolynski No. 230
Nowo-Ingermanljandski No. 10
Nowo-Ladoshski No. 436
Nowomoskowski No. 281
Nowooskolski No. 314
Noworshewski No. 269
Nowotorshski No. 114
Nowtoroizko-Jakaterinoslawski No. 4
Nowo-Trokski No. 169
Nowotscherkasski No. 145
Nowousenski No. 328
Nowydworski No. 456

Obdorski No. 483
Obojanski No. 332
Ochotski No. 43
Ochtski No. 438
Odesski No. 48
Odojewski No. 223
Okski No. 321
Olgopolski No. 259
Olonezki No. 14
Olwiopolski No. 499
Omski No. 96
Oneshski No. 90
Orenburgski No. 105
Orgjewski No. 498
Orlowski No. 36
Orowajski No. 195
Orski No. 331
Ostaschkowski No. 216
Ostrogoshski No. 488
Ostrolenski No. 181
Ostroshski No. 167
Ostrowski No. 100
Otschakowski No. 190
Owrutschski No. 309

Pawlogradski No. 283
Pensenski No. 121
Perejaslawski No. 277
Perekopski No. 253
Perewolotschenski No. 176
Permski No. 101
Petrosawodski No. 103
Petrowski No. 88
Petschorski No. 92
Pirjatinski No. 451
Pjatigorski No. 151
Podolski No. 55
Polozki No. 28
Poltawski No. 30
Ponechowski No. 455
Porchowski No. 413
Porjetschenski No. 266
Poschechonski No. 268
Potijski No. 201
Potschaewski No. 506
Powjnezki No. 426
Pragski No. 58
Pskowski No. 1
Pudosheski No. 427
Pultuski No. 183
Putiwlski No. 127

Radomyslski No. 232
Ralinsky No. 474
Rewelski No. 7
Rishski No. 429
Rishski No. 2 (Latvian)
Rjasanski No. 69

Rjashski No. 70
Rjeshitzki No.507
Romanowski No. 212
Romanski No. 475
Romenski No. 174
Roslawlski No. 221
Rownenski No. 166
Rshewski No. 490
Rybinski No. 489
Rylski No. 126
Rymnikski No. 192

Sadomski No. 28
Sakatalski No. 164
Saljanski No. 206
Samarski No. 147
Samostski No. 60
Samurski No. 83
Saraiski No. 140
Saranski No. 407
Sarapulski No. 501
Saratowski No. 108
Saslawski No. 300
Schatilowski No.671
Schatski No. 310
Schemachinski No. 205
Schirwanski No. 84
Schlisselburgski No. 15
Schtschigrowski No. 406
Schuiski No. 118
Scbeshski No. 544
Selenski No. 686
Selenginski No. 41
Semgalski Nr. 5 (Latvian)
Semljandski No. 226
Serdobski No. 420
Serpuchowski No. 120
Sestrojezki No. 437
Sewastopolski No. 75
Shisdrinski No. 482
Shitomirski No.56
Siedellezki No, 241
Siligerski No. 464
Simbirski No. 24
Simferopolski No. 133
Sitschervski No. 511
Sjenenski No. 303
Sjenver-Donetzki No. 547
Sjewski No. 34
Skopinski No. 20
Skwirski No.229
Slatoustski No. 330
Slawjanoserbski No. 248
Slawjanski No. 412
Smijewski No. 450
Smolenski No. 25
Sofijski No. 2
Soligalitschski No. 322
Solvrvytschegodski No. 552
Sosninski No. 443
Spasski No.307
Starizki No. 462
Starobjelski No. 233
Starokonstantinowski No. 505
Starooskolski No. 128
Starorusski No. 113
Strawropolski No. 74
Stawutschanski No. 251
Subzowski No. 461
Sucharewski No. 215
Suchinitschski No. 540
Suchumski No. 203
Sudshanski No. 458
Sumskoi No. 411
Surashski No. 302
Surski No. 280
Susdalski No. 62
Swenigorodski No. 142
Swijahski No. 193
Swirki No. 295

Taganrogski No. 136
Tamanski No. 150
Tambowski No. 122
Tarusski No. 287
Tarutinski No. 67
Tatarski No.67
Temnikowski No. 445
Tenginski No. 77
Tichwinski No. 431
Timski No. 460
Tiraspolski No. 131
Tobolski No. 38
Tomski No. 39
Toropetzki No.414
Torshokski No. 478
Troizki Nr. 107
Troizo-Sergiewski No. 194
Trubtschewski No. 291
Tscheboksarski No. 308
Tscheljabinski No. 336
Tschembarski No. 320
Tscherepowjezki No. 434
Tscherkassi No. 508
Tschernigowski No. 29
Tschernojarski No. 318
Tschernomorski No. 149
Tschistopolski No. 502
Tschigirinski No. 503Tschudskoi No. 424
Tukkumski No. 6 (Latvian)
Tulski No. 72
Twerski No. 441

Ufimski No. 106
Uglizki No. 63
Ukrainski No.47
Uralski No. 112
Urshumski No.465
Usmanski No. 410
Ust-Dwinski No. 179

Ust-Dwinski No. 1 (Latvian)
Ust-Pineshski No. 515
Ustjushski No. 104
Ustjushski No. 213
Ust-Medwjedizki No. 402

Waldaiski No. 432
Walksi No. 430
Walujski No. 290
Warnawinski No. 491
Warschawski No. 184
Wasilkowski No. 312
Wawrski No. 240
Welikoluzki No. 12
Weliko Ustjuschski No. 551
Welishski No. 531
Wendenski No. 178
Wengrowski No. 284
Werchnednjeprowski No. 416
Werchneuralski No. 504
Wetlushski No. 238
Widsemski No. 4 (Latvian)
Wilejski No. 363
Wilenski No. 52
Wilkomirski No. 496
Wilmanstrandski No. 86
Windawski No. 180
Witebski No. 27
Wjasemski No. 115
Wjatski No. 102
Wjerejski No. 494
Wladikawkaski No. 152
Wladimirski No. 61
Wolchowski No. 510
Wolmarski No. 8 (Latvian)
Wologodski No. 18
Wolshski No. 109
Wolski No. 403
Woltschanski No. 546
Wolynski No. 53
Woroneshski No. 124
Wyborgski No. 85
Wyschnewolozki No. 265
Wysokolitowski No. 394

Zarewski No. 325
Zarizynski No. 146
Zarskoselski No. 421
Zninski No. 446

Grenadier Infantry Regiments(Grenadjérski polk)
Astrachanski No. 12
Eriwanski No.13
Fanagorijski No. 11
Grusinski No. 14
Jekaterinoslawski No. 1
Kiewski No.5
Malorossijski No. 10
Mingrelski No. 16
Moskowski No. 8
Neswishski No. 4
Pernowski No. 3
Rostowski No. 2
Samogitski No. 7
Siberski No. 9
Tawritscheski No. 6
Tifliski No. 15

Border Guard/Patrol Regiments
Kalischski No. 2
Rishski No. 3
Njemenski No. 4
Rypinski No. 1
Taurogenski No. 6

Mounted Regiments (Kónny polk)
Dagestanski No.1 and No. 2
Ingushski (Caucasian)
Kabardinski (Caucasian)
Krymski
Ossetinski
Proskurower No. 1
Tatarski (Caucasian)
Tscherkesski (Caucasian)
Turkmenski
Tschernomorski
Tschetschenski (Caucasian)

Mounted Border Guard/Patrol Regiments (Kónny polk)
Baltijski No. 1-3
Chotinski No. 19
Gorschdinski No. 5
Grajewski No. 6
Kalischski No. 12
Lomshinski No. 9
Rypinski
Sandmirski No. 15
Tomaschewski No. 17

Lifeguard Infantry Regiments (Lejbgwardjéjskaja polk)
Finljandski
Grenaderski
Ismailowski
Jegerski
Kexholmski
Moskowski
Pawlowski
Petrogradski
Preobrashenski
Semjonowski
Wolynski

Lifeguard Cavalry Regiments (Gwardjéjskaja kawaleriskaja polk)
Chevalier
Grodnenski (Hussar)
Kurljandski No. 2 (Uláanski)

Cossack Regiments (Kazatschi-polk)
Amurski Cossack Regiments No. 1 and No. 3
Argunski Trans-Siberian/Transbaikal Cossack Regiments No. 1 and No. 2
Atamanski Grand Cossack Regiment
Choperski Kuban Cossack Regiments No.1, No, 2 and No. 3
Gorsko-Mosdoski Terek Cossack Regiment No.1,No.2, and No.3
Isetsko-Strawropolski Orenburg Cossack No. 4
Jekaterinodarski Kuban Cossack Regiment No.1, No.2, and No.3
Kawkaski Kuban Cossack Regiment No. 1, No.2, and No.3
Kisljaro-Grebenski Terek Cossack Regiment No.1,No.2, and No.3
Kubanski Cossack Regiment No.1, No.2, and No.3
Labinski Cossack Regiment No. 1, No.2, and No.3
Linejny Kuban Cossack Regiment No. 1, No.2, and No.3
Nertschinski Trans Siberian/Transbaikal Cossack Regiment No. 1 and No. 2
Poltawski Kuban Cossack Regiment No. 1, No.2, and No.3
Saporoshski Kuban Cossack Regiment No. 1, No.2, and No.3
Semirjetschenski Cossack Regiment No. 1, No.2, and No.3
Sibirski Cossack Regiments No.1 – No. 10
Sundsha-Wladikawkaski Terek Cossack Regiment No.1,No.2, and No.3
Tamanski Kuban Cossack Regiment No. 1, No.2, and No.3
Tschernomorski Kuban Cossack Regiment No. 1, No.2, and No.3
Tschistinski Trans Siberian/Transbaikal Cossack Regiment No. 1 and No. 2
Ufimsko-Samarski Orenburg Cossack Regiment No. 3
Umanski Kuban Cossack Regiment No. 1, No.2, and No.3
Ussurijiski Cossack Regiment
Werchne-Udinski Trans Siberian/Transbaikal Cossack Regiment No. 1, No. 2 and No. 3
Wolgski Terek Cossack Regiment No.1,No.2, and No.3

Hussar Regiments (Huzárski polk)
Achtyrski No. 12
Alexandrijski No. 5
Bjelorusski Nr. 7
Ingermanljandski No. 10
Irkutski No. 16
Isjumski No. 11
Jelisawetgradski No. 3
Kiewski No. 9
Kljastizki No. 6
Lubenski No. 8
Mariupolski No. 4
Mitawski No.14
Narwski No. 13
Njeshinski No. 18
Pawlogradski No. 2
Sumski No. 1
Tschernigowski No.17
Ukrainski No. 15

Dragoon Regiments (Dragùnski polk)
Archangelogorodski No. 19
Astrachanski No. 8
Finljandski No. 20
Gluchowski No. 6
Kargopolski No. 5
Kasanski No. 9
Kinburnski No. 7
Malorossijski No. 14
Nishegorodski No. 17
Noworossijski No. 3
Nowtoroizko-Jakaterinoslawski No. 4
Perejaslawski No. 15
Primorski No.
Pskowski No. 2
Rishski No. 11
Sjewerski No. 18
Starodubowski No. 12

Tschernigowski No. 51
Twerski No. No. 16
Wojennawo Ordena No. 13

Lancer (Ulánski polk) Regiments
Bjelgorooski No. 12
Bugski No. 9
Charkowski No. 4
Jamburgski No. 14
Litowski No. 5
Nowoarchangelski No. 16
Nowomirgorodski No. 17
Odesski No. 10
Olwiopolski No. 7
Petrogradski No. 1
Smolenski No.3
Tatarski No. 15
Tschugujewski No. 11
Wladimirski No. 13
Wolynski No.6
Wosnjesenski No. 8

Appendix Two

The Composition of the Czarist Russian Armed Forces in 1917

(This chart has been translated and adapted from a chart compiled by the High Command of the k.u.k (imperial and royal) or Austro-Hungarian Armed Forces in 1917)

Ethnic Origin, Religious Beliefs, and Language Capabilities.	**Approximate Population and Regions Inhabited. *Total population of Russia in 1917 Ca. 180,000,000**	**Characteristics of Military Service**
Abchasian Islam / Greek Orthodox Minority Abchasian	Ca. 72,000 Military District located in Suchum near the Black Sea in Kuban territory.	Were not required to do Military Service until the First World War.
Adighe Islam Adighian and Tscherkessian	Ca. 100,000 Lower and Middle Kuban River Valley.	Were not required to do Military Service until the First World War.
Armenian Gregorian Church/ Greek Orthodox Armenian	1,674,000 Trans Caucus (Kars, Alexandropol, Eriwan, Sarykamysch)	Compulsory Military Service. Served as Volunteers, Riflemen and Mounted Troops.
Avaren Islam Avarian	Southwest region of the Dagestan territory	Were not required to do Military Service until the First World War.
Baschirian Sunni Islam Baschirian, Tartar and Russian	Ca. 2,000,000 Southern Ural and the Bjelaja and Ufa Basin	Compulsory Military Service. Served as Volunteers, Riflemen and Mounted Troops. Excellent horsemen.
Bulgarian Greek Orthodox Bulgarian and Russian	Ca. 252,000 Bessarabia, Taurien, Trans Caucus.	Compulsory Military Service. Cited often for bravery.
Burjaeten Lamaism / Greek Orthodox. Burjaetian and Russian.	Ca. 380,000 The mountainous region around the Bajkal Lake and in the southern Irkutsk region.	Were not required to do Military Service until the First World War.
Czechs Roman Catholic/ Greek Orthodox Czech and Russian	Ca. 70,000 In Wolhynien, Podolien, the southeast coast of the Black Sea and in the Caucus	Compulsory Military Service. Exceptional Artillerist.
Cheremissian Greek Orthodox Cheremissian and Russian	Ca. 540,000 On the banks of the Volga. Also, in Wjatka and Kasan	Compulsory Military Service.

Chechnyian Islam Chechnyian	Ca. 300,000 In the areas of Vladikawkas, Petropawlowsk, Chassaw, and Jurt. The provinces of Tiflis and Terek.	Were not required to do Military Service until the First World War. Served in Mounted Regiments.
Dunganian Islam Chinese, Tartar and Russian	Ca. 10,000 Northwestern regions. Kuldscha.	Were not required to do Military Service until the First World War.
Estonian Greek Orthodox / Protestant. Estonian	Ca. 1,440,000 Estonia and the Baltic States/Countries	Compulsory Military Service. Cited often for bravery and regarded as elite troops. Served in Guard and Grenadier Regiments. Also, served in Marine or Naval service.
Finnish Protestant Finnish	Ca. 2,000,000 Finland and Petrograd	Cited often for bravery and regarded as elite troops. Served in Guard and Grenadier Regiments
Georgian Greek Orthodox / Catholic Georgian and Russian	Ca. 600,000 Throughout the Caucus.	Compulsory Military Service. Cited often for bravery and regarded as elite troops. Served as Volunteers, Riflemen and Mounted Troops.
German Catholic/ Protestant German and Russian	Ca. 2,556,000 Found throughout the Empire.	Compulsory Military Service.
Greek Greek Orthodox Greek and Russian	Ca. 50,000 Coastal Cities on the Black Sea and in the Crimea	Compulsory Military Service.
"Great /Large" Russian Orthodox Russian	Ca. 79,740,000 Found throughout the Empire.	Compulsory Military Service.
Immeretian Greek Orthodox Georgian	Ca. 530,000 Around Kutais	Compulsory Military Service. Cited often for bravery and regarded as elite troops. Served as Volunteers, Riflemen and Mounted Troops.
Jakutian Greek orthodox/Shamanism Jakutian	Ca. 324,000 Chatanga	Were not required to do Military Service until the First World War.
J (Y) ezedi Various religious beliefs Jezedian and Kurdish	Population Unknown Eriwan and the Caucus	Were not required to do Military Service until the First World War.
Jewish Hebrew and Russian as well as other languages	Ca. 7,254,000 Found throughout the Empire.	Compulsory Military Service.
Karbardian Islam / Greek Orthodox Minority Karbardian, AdigheP Dialects and Tscherkessian	Ca. 80,000 The mountainous region in the Northern Caucus. East Circassian.	Were not required to do Military Service until the First World War. "Karbardinski" Mounted Regiment.

Kalmuekian Greek Orthodox, Buddhism and Shamanism Kalmuekian	Ca. 300,000 The regions between the Volga, Don and Manytsch River and in Semrjetschensk Territory	Were not required to do Military Service until the First World War. Nomadic Herdsmen.
Kamtshadalian Greek Orthodox Kamtshadalian and Russian	Ca. 4000 Southern part of the Kamtshatka peninsula and on the Island of Schumschu	Were not required to do Military Service until the First World War.
Karaitian Sect of Judaism Karaitian	Ca. 5,000 The Crimea and in the vicinity of Simferopol.	Compulsory Military Service.
Karelian Greek Orthodox Russian	Ca. 300,000 South East Finland	Compulsory Military Service.
Kirgisian Sunni Islam Kirgisisch	Ca. 5,832,000 Southwestern Siberia, Northern Trans Caspian and Turkestan.	Were not required to do Military Service until the First World War.
Korean Buddhism Korean	Ca. 15,000 Russian Territory in Eastern Siberia	Compulsory Military Service.
Koryakian Greek Orthodox / Shamanism Koryakian	Ca. 4,500 In the regions of Gishiga and Penshina.	Were not required to do Military Service until the First World War.
Kumueks Islam Kumuekian	Ca.80,000 In the regions between the Terek and Sulak Rivers and along the coast of the Caspian Sea from Chassaw-Jurt-Petrowsk to Derbent.	Compulsory Military Service. Served as Volunteers, Riflemen and Mounted Troops. Excellent horsemen. 1st and 2nd Daghestan Mounted Regiment.
Kurds Sunni Islam Kurdish	Ca. 85,000 Caucus, eastern Eriwan and the borderlands of Turkey and Persia.	Were not required to do Military Service.
Kwaenen Greek Orthodox Russian	Ca. 100,000 South East Finland. Karelia.	Were not required to do Military Service until the First World War.
Laplander or Lapps Greek Orthodox / Evangelical Lapp	Population Unknown Northern Finland. Archangelsk and Olonez.	Compulsory Military Service. Marine or Naval Service.
Lasen Islam Lasish	Ca. 60,000 Along the coast of the Black Sea.	Were not required to do Military Service until the First World War.
Lesghierian Islam Lesgish	Ca. 600,000 Northeastern regions in the Caucus. Baku and Jelisawetpol.	Compulsory Military Service. Cited often for bravery. 1st and 2nd Daghestan Mounted Regiment.
Latvian Greek Orthodox / Catholic / Protestant Latvian and Russian	Ca. 2,052,000 Latvia, Kurland and the Baltic States/ Countries.	Compulsory Military Service. Cited often for bravery and regarded as elite troops. Served as Volunteers, Riflemen, Mounted Troops and in Marine or Naval service

Lithuanian Roman Catholic and Greek Orthodox. Lithuanian	Ca. 1,728,000 Baltic States/Countries.	Compulsory Military Service. Cited often for bravery and regarded as elite troops.
Liven Protestant Livish	Ca. 4,000 Baltic coast and the Kurland peninsula.	Compulsory Military Service. Cited often for bravery and regarded as elite troops. Served as Volunteers, Riflemen, Mounted Troops and in Marine or Naval service
Meschtsherjaekian Islam Meschtsherjaekian, Baschirian and Russian	Ca. 140,000 Ufa, Orenburg and Pensa	Compulsory Military Service.
Mingrel Catholic and Greek Orthodox Mingrel and Georgian	Ca. 300,000 On the Black Sea between Abchasia and the Rion River. Also in Odischi and Gurien.	Compulsory Military Service
Mordwinian Greek Orthodox Mordwinian	Ca. 1,458,000 Simbirsk, Nizhni-Novogorod, Saratow, Tambow, Pensa, and Samara.	Compulsory Military Service. Cited often for bravery and regarded as elite troops
Nogaierian Islam Nogaierian	Ca. 18,000 Stawropol and Terek territories.	Were not required to do Military Service until the First World War.
Ossetian (Osset) Greek Orthodox and Islam Ossetian (Osset)	Ca. 200,000 Northern and Central Caucus. Ossetia	Compulsory Military Service Ossetian Mounted Regiment and Ossetian Plastuni Battalion.
Ostjacian Greek Orthodox and Shamanism Ostjacian	Ca. 23,000 Tobolsk, Tomsk and Jenissejsk	Were not required to do Military Service until the First World War.
Permian Greek Orthodox Permian	Ca. 70,000 Perm and Wjatka	Compulsory Military Service
Persian (Iranian) Islam Persian	Ca. 20,000 Amu-Darja Territory, Caspian Sea Region and Southern Russia.	Were not required to do Military Service until the First World War.
Poles Roman Catholic and Protestant Polish	Ca. 11,358,000 Poland/Russia	Compulsory Military Service. Cited often for bravery. Especially, Polish Lancers (*Ulański*).
Rome Various religious beliefs Rome and other languages	Ca. 200,000 Nomadic. Found largely in Bessarabia.	Compulsory Military Service. Excelled as Military Musicians and Craftsman.
Rumanian Orthodox Rumanian	Ca. 750,000 Bessarabia, Dnjester, Cherson and Jekaterinoslaw.	Compulsory Military Service
Samojedian Greek Orthodox and Shamanism Samojedian	Ca. 30,000 Ufer, Petschora, and Jenissej	Were not required to do Military Service.
Sarten Islam Persian, Uzbek, and Turkmen	Ca. 1,300,000 In Turkestan	Were not required to do Military Service until the First World War.

Serbs Greek Orthodox Serbian and Russian	Ca. 12,000 Cherson and Jekaterinoslaw	Compulsory Military Service. Highly intelligent and very brave soldiers.
"Small/Little" Russia (Ukrainian, Ruthenian, Malorussi) Catholic/Greek Orthodox Small/Little" Russian / Ruthenian	Ca. 32,058,000 Southwest Russia and the eastern coast of the Azowschen Sea	Compulsory Military Service. Excellent horsemen.
Sojotian Buddhism Sojotian	Ca. 14,000 Altai and the Sajanian Mountains	Were not required to do Military Service.
Svantian Greek Orthodox Svantian and Russian	Ca. 15,000 Trans Caucus region	Compulsory Military Service.
Syrian Orthodox Syrian	Ca. 290,000 Vologda, Vytschegda and Petschora.	Compulsory Military Service. Excelled as marksmen and mounted artillerists.
Tadschikian Islam Persian and Uzbek	Ca. 630,000 Samarkand and Chodshent	Were not required to do Military Service until the First World War.
Volga Tartars Islam Tartar	Ca. 5,346,000 **On the Volga**, in the Crimea, in Siberia and in the Caucus.	Were not required to do Military Service until the First World War.
Crimean Tartars Islam Tartar	Ca. 5,346,000 On the Volga, **in the Crimea**, in Siberia and in the Caucus.	Compulsory Military Service. Excellent horsemen and regarded as elite troops.
Siberian Tartars Greek Orthodox and Islam Tartar	Ca. 5,346,000 On the Volga, in the Crimea, **in Siberia** and in the Caucus.	Were not required to do Military Service until the First World War.
Caucasian Tartars Islam Tartar	On the Volga, in the Crimea, in Siberia and **in the Caucus**	Were not required to do Military Service until the First World War. Served as Mounted
Volunteers. Tekinzian (Tekke-Turkmenian) Sunni Islam Turkmen	Population Unknown Karacum Desert	Were not required to do Military Service until the First World War.
Teptjaerian Islam Tartar	Ca. 500,000 Orenburg, Samara, and Ufa	Compulsory Military Service.
Tscherkessian Greek Orthodox and Islam Tscherkessian	Ca. 300,000 In the Northern Caucus as well as in Kuban and Terek territories.	Christians: Compulsory Military Service Muslims: Were not required to do Military Service until the First World War.
Tschuden Greek Orthodox Finnish and Russian	Ca. 20,000 In Ladoga, Onega, and Bjelojesees.	Compulsory Military Service

Tschuktschian Greek Orthodox and Shamanism Tschuktschian	Ca. 20,000 Tschuktsch Peninsula	Were not required to do Military Service.
Tschuwaschian Greek Orthodox and Islam Tschuwaschian	Ca. 1,206,000 Simbirsk, Samara, and Ufa	Compulsory Military Service Excellent marksmen and horsemen.
Tungusian Shamanism Tungusian	Ca. 90,000 Eastern Siberia	Were not required to do Military Service.
Turkmen Sunni Islam Turkmen	Ca. 1,170, 000 In the desert between Amu-Darja and the Caspian Sea.	Were not required to do Military Service until the First World War.
Uzbek Islam Uzbek	Ca. 1,044,000 Ferghana-Syr-Darjageb, Sarafschan, Kuldscha and Amu-Darja	Were not required to do Military Service until the First World War.
Vogulian Greek Orthodox and Shamanism Vogulian	Ca. 35,000 The Northern Ural Mountains	Were not required to do Military Service until the First World War.
Votjakian Greek Orthodox Votjakian	Ca. 594,000 Wjatka, Kasan and Perm	Compulsory Military Service
White Russian (Belarus/ Bjelo-Russi) Greek Orthodox and Catholic White Russian	Ca. 8,420,000 The forested terrain between Djeper-Pripiatj and the upper western Dwina	Compulsory Military Service Excellent marksmen and horsemen.

Appendix Three

Czarist Russian Artillery in 1917

(This chart has been translated and adapted from a chart compiled by the High Command of the k.u.k. (imperial and royal)or Austro-Hungarian Armed Forces in 1917)

Models, Calibers, and Names of Artillery Pieces	Usage and Deployment
2" (6.5cm) Balloon busters and anti-aircraft cannons	Anti-aircraft
3" (7.62 cm) Field cannon M. 1902 Putilov	Mounted (as well as motorized) Artillery
3" (7.62 cm) Howitzer (Mountain Artillery) M. 1904 Obuchov	Foot and Mounted Artillery
3" (7.62 cm) Howitzer (Mountain Artillery) M. 1909 Schneider-Danglis	Foot and Mounted Artillery
48" (12.19 cm) Artillery piece M. 1909 Krupp	Mortar/Artillery
48" (12.19 cm) Artillery piece M. 1910 Schneider	Mortar/Artillery
42" (10.68 cm) Field cannon L/35 M.77	Heavy Field Artillery
42" (10.68 cm) Field cannon M. 1913 Schneider	Heavy Field Artillery
6" (15 cm) Field Cannon M.77	Heavy Field Artillery
6" (15 cm) Field Cannon M. 1910 (Schneider System)	Heavy Field Artillery

6" (15 cm) Field Cannon M.77	Siege Artillery
6" (15 cm) Field Cannon M. 1904	Siege Artillery
8" (20 cm) Field Cannon L/15 M. 77	Siege Artillery
6" (15 cm) Mortar M. 86	Siege Artillery
8" (20 cm) Mortar M. 87	Siege Artillery
9" (20 cm) Mortar M. 87	Siege Artillery
11" (28cm) Mortar (Schneider System)	Siege Artillery

Glossary

Aboróna	Defense
Adjélnaja kawaleriskaja brigade	Independent Cavalry Brigade
Adjélnaja gwardjéjskaja kawaleriskaja brigade	Independent Guard Cavalry Brigade
Adjélnaja donskája-kazátschaja brigade	Independent Don Cossack Brigade
Adjélnaja pjechótnaja - brigáda assóbowo-naznatschénia	Independent Infantry Brigade for special intended purposes or operations.
Adjélnaja morskája –brigáda	Independent Marine Brigade
Adjélnaja donskája-kazátschaja sotnja	Independent Don Cossack Squad
Adjélny assádny artileríjski diwizión	Independent Siege Artillery Division
Adjélna sapiórnaja-róta	Independent Pioneer Company
Adjélnaja telegráfnaja-róta	Independent Telegraph Company
Akóp	Trenches, dugouts, bunkers
Am?rskij kazatschi-polk	Amurian Cossack Regiment
Apoltschénskaja diwízia	Reserve/ National Guard Division
Apoltschénski pjechótny polk	Reserve/ National Guard Infantry Regiment
Apoltschénski kawaleríski polk	Reserve /National Guard Cavalry Regiment
Apoltschénskaja sapjórnaja polróta	Reserve/National Guard Pioneer Regiment
Ármija	Army
Armjéjski kórpus	Army Corp
Armjéjskaja	Infantry (Army)
Armiéjskij awiaziónny atrjád	Army Air Force Squadron/Detachment
Artileriskaja brigáda	Artillery brigade
Assádny artileríski-polk	Siege Artillery Regiment
Ataman	Commander and Chief of the Cossacks Literal translations - Father of male warriors or Father of Horsemen.
Atáka polewói ukrjepljónnoi posícii	Attack a fortified position
Awiaziónnaja róta	Air Corps / Flight Company
Awtomobílnaja pulemjótnaja róta	Automobile/Mobil Machinegun Company
Bashlik	A hood or cowl normally made of wool. It was secured by the shoulder boards on the overcoat and waist belt.
Batalión	Battalion
Bateréja	Battery
Batyushka	Regimental Priest
Bebóut	A curved knife. These knives were preferred by scouts and artillerists
Belyo	linen, or literal translation, that which is white. Many gymnastoirka were made of linen, particularly earlier models.
Bojewói poriádok	Command Post
Brigáda	Brigade
Diwizión	Division
Dragùnski polk	Dragoon Regiment
Front jugozápadny	Southwestern Front
Front sjéwerny	Northern Front
Front západny	West Front
Frontovik	Front line soldier
Frontoviki	Frontline Troops
Furashka	Field Cap or Visor Cap

Gaziri	Cossack/Caucasian cartridges. Usually made of silver and carried in the chest pouches on Tcherkessa (long coat).
Gory diwizión	Mountain Artillery Division
Grenadjérski kórpus	Grenadier Corps
Grenadjérskaja (pjechótnaja) diwízia	Grenadier (Infantry) Division
Grenadjérski (pjechótny) polk	Grenadier (Infantry) Regiment
Gwardjéski kórpus	Guard Corps
Gwardjéski kawaleríski kórpus	Guard Cavalry Corps
Gwardjéjskaja kawaleriskaja diwízia	Guard Cavalry Division
Gwardjéjskaja kawaleriskaja brigáda	Guard Cavalry Brigade
Gwardjéjskaja pjechóta	Guard Infantry
Gwardjéjskaja pjechótnaja diwízia	Guard Infantry Division
Gymnastiorka	Field Blouse/Shirt/Tunic. Literal translation—sport or training washable
Iskrowaja róta	Field Communications (Telephone/Telegraph) Company
Kawaleríski kórpus (diwízia)	Cavalry Corps (Division)
Kawalergárdski polk	Chevalier Guard Regiment
Kawkáskaja armjéjski- kórpus	Caucasian Army Corps
Khlopok	Cotton. Many gymnastoirka were made of cotton.
Khorunzhiy	A rank for officers in Cossack Regiments
Kinjal	double edged knife preferred by Cossacks
Kirassírski polk	Cuirassier Regiment
Kitel	officer's wool tunic
Kónnaja diwízia	Mounted division
Kónno-artileríski diwízion	Mounted/Horse Artillery Division
Kónno-górny artileríski diwízion	Mounted/Horse Mountain Artillery Division
Kónny polk	Mounted Regiment
Kortik	A dagger or dirk
Kosh	A Cossack camp or troop
Krjépostny artileríski polk (batalión)	Fortress Artillery Regiment (Battalion)
Krushka/Krushki	Mess kit(s). Normally copper with the inside tinned.
Kubánski kasátschi-polk	Kuban Cossack Regiment
Kwartíra	Quarters
Morskói polk	Marine Regiment
Morskói artileríski diwízion	Marine Artillery Division
Mortírny artileríski diwízion	Mortar Artillery Division
Nastuplénie	Attack or Advance
Orden Andreia Pervozvannogo	The Order of St. Andrew. The highest Russian Award, which was usually reserved for nobility.
Orden Svjatoi Alexandra Nevskogo	The Order St. Alexander Nevsky. This decoration was instituted by Empress Catherine I in 1725.
Orden Svjatoi Vladimira	The Order of St. Vladimir. This decoration was instituted by Empress Catherine I in 1783.
Orden Belogo Orla	The Order of the White Eagle. Originally a Polish order, it became an Imperial Order when Russia absorbed Poland into her Empire.
Otstuplénje	Retreat or Withdraw
Papaha	Fur/Fleece Caps or Astrakhan
Perewóska	Transport
Pilótka	Pillbox shaped hat. Forage Cap.
Pjechóta	Infantry
Plastùni	Forward scouts/Infantry, usually Cossacks
Pogoni	Shoulder Boards
Polk	Regiment
Polkovnik	Roughly equivalent to the rank of Colonel. This term also describes a Commander of a Cossack regiment.
Polijewája wozducho-pláwatelnaja róta	Field Balloon Company
Polijewoí shandármski eskadrón	Field Gendarme (Military Police) Squad
Polushubok	a long overcoat with a large chest pocket that buttons shut.
Pontónny batalión	Pontoon Battalion
Pulemjót	Machinegun
Pulemjótnaja róta	Machinegun Company

Pulemjótny awtomobílny wzwod	Mobil/Automobile Machinegun platoon
Pulya	Bullet
Róta	Company
Rugjë	rifle
Sapogi	Boots
Shashka	Saber
Sheljésno doróshny batalión	Railroad Battalion
Shinel	Heavy wool gray overcoat
Sotnik	A captain of a company. This terms was usually used by Cossacks.
STAVKA	High Command of the Armed Forces
Stanitsa	A Cossack village
Svjatoi Georggi Orden	The Order of St. George. St. George Cross for Valor
Svjatoi Ekateriny Orden	The Order of St. Catherine. This decoration had two classes and was reserved for ladies.
Svjatoi Anny Orden	The Order of St. Anne. This was originally a civilian decoration, but became a military decoration. The military decoration has two crossed swords.
Svjatoi Stanislava Orden	The Order St. Stanislaus. Originally instituted by King Stanislaus II in 1765. It became accepted as an Order in Russia.
Tsashóly artileríski diwízion	Heavy Artillery Division
Tcherkessa	The Cossack/Caucasian long coat or tunic
Udár w schtyky	Bayonet Attack
Ukrjepljóny	fortified/entrenched
Ulánski polk	Ulan/Lancer Regiment
Ushanka	Similar to a papaha, but normally with ear flaps that folded down for protection in harsh weather
Voiskos	Standing Army
Volba	Dried fish. A classic Russian dish that was also used by soldiers as rations
Vzvod	Platoon
Yasaul	A rank for officers in Cossack regiments

Further Reading

Table of Uniforms Worn by the Russian Army in 1910. V. K. Schenk. 1910. Russia.

The Shadow of the Winter Palace.: Russia's Drift to Revolution 1825-1917. Edward Crankshaw. Viking Press. New York. 1976.

The Russian People in 1914. Chronicles from National Geographic. Arthur M. Schlesinger, Jr., Senior Consulting Editor and Fred L. Israel, General Editor. Chelsea House Publishers. Philadelphia. 2000.

The Orders of Russia. V.A. Durov. Moscow. 1993

August 1914. Alexander Solzhenitsyn. (Translated by Michael Glenny). Farrar, Straus and Giroux. New York. 1971.

A History of Russia. George Vernadsky. Revised Edition. New Home Library. New York. 1944.

The Guns of August. Barbara W. Tuchman. Dell Publishing. New York.
1962.

Die Russische Armee Anfang. 1917. k.u.k Hof-Staatsdruckerei, Vienna, Austria. 1917.

Uniforms & Equipment of the Austro-Hungarian Army in World War One

Spencer A. Coil

Franz Joseph I and Karl. These emperors ruled a multiethnic empire destined to become one of the central powers in World War I. In addition to the studio portraits shown, the candid photos offer an authentic view of life in the trenches and on the battlefield. Each photo has been carefully chosen and researched to offer the reader detailed information on the *k.u.k* (royal and imperial) Empire's air, motor and medical corps, as well as infantry, artillery, pioneer and railroad troops. There are chapters covering highly decorated elite units, such as the Bosnian and the *Kaiserschuetzen*. A full color section of heretofore unpublished photos of original head dress, uniforms, equipment and accessories used by the k.u.k armed forces provides valuable information on the materials, markings, stamps, and construction of field caps, cavalry helmets and flight gear. Also included in this section are pilot badges and cap and collar insignia. This book is an indispensable resource for all historians, collectors, re-enactors, war gamers and model builders.

Size: 9" x 12" ■ over 550 black and white and color photographs ■ 352 pp

ISBN: 0-7643-1869-1 ■ hard cover ■ $69.95